Aquatic vegetation and its use and control

Aquatic vegetation and its use and control

Edited by D. S. Mitchell

A contribution to the International Hydrological Decade

Unesco   Paris   1974

Published by the United Nations
Educational, Scientific and Cultural Organization,
Place de Fontenoy, 75700 Paris

Printed by Imprimerie Louis - Jean, Gap

ISBN 92-3-101082-4

Preface

The International Hydrological Decade (IHD) 1965-74 was launched by the General Conference of Unesco at its thirteenth session to promote international co-operation in research and studies and the training of specialists and technicians in scientific hydrology. Its purpose is to enable all countries to make a fuller assessment of their water resources and a more rational use of them as man's demands for water constantly increase in face of developments in population, industry and agriculture. In 1972, national committees for the Decade had been formed in 107 of Unesco's 130 Member States to carry out national activities and to contribute to regional and international activities within the programme of the Decade. The implementation of the programme is supervised by a Co-ordinating Council, composed of thirty Member States selected by the General Conference of Unesco, which studies proposals for developments of the programme, recommends projects of interest to all or a large number of countries, assists in the development of national and regional projects and co-ordinates international co-operation.

Promotion of collaboration in developing hydrological research techniques, diffusing hydrological data and planning hydrological installations is a major feature of the programme of the IHD which encompasses all aspects of hydrological studies and research. Hydrological investigations are encouraged at the national, regional and international level to strengthen and to improve the use of natural resources from a local and a global perspective. The programme provides a means for countries well advanced in hydrological research to exchange scientific views and for developing countries to benefit from this exchange of information in elaborating research projects and in implementing recent developments in the planning of hydrological installations.

As part of Unesco's contribution to the achievement of the objectives of the IHD the General Conference authorized the Director-General to collect, exchange and disseminate information concerning research on scientific hydrology and to facilitate contacts between research workers in this field. To this end, Unesco has published a number of studies, including twenty-seven volumes already issued within the two series *Studies and Reports in Hydrology* and *Technical Papers in Hydrology,* and also various miscellaneous publications.

The responsibility for the choice and presentation of facts and for opinions and views expressed lies with the authors cited in each volume.

The designations employed and the presentation of the material do not imply the expression of any opinion whatsoever on the part of Unesco concerning the legal status of any country or territory, or of its authorities, or concerning the frontiers of any country or territory.

Contents

Foreword

Since its inception in 1965, the Co-ordinating Council for the IHD has studied the control and possible eradication of nuisance aquatic plants in view of the fact that the relationship between plants and hydrology has significant implications in many fields: agriculture, irrigation, fisheries, wildlife conservation, public health, recreation, flood control, drainage and inland navigation. In 1967 the Council invited the International Biological Programme (IBP) to collaborate with the IHD Secretariat in the preparation of an international programme, and subsequently an *ad hoc* panel of experts was set up on the ecology and control of aquatic vegetation. This panel proposed that studies be made on the ecology of water weeds in fresh and brackish waters and non-oceanic bodies, and that countries having a problem of excessive vegetation analyse the problem with a view to finding suitable methods of control. The panel also suggested that a manual be prepared for the identification of aquatic plants—particularly those found in tropical areas—and Unesco financed a mission which was undertaken by Professor Cook of the University of Zürich in order to collect material for that manual, which is at present in preparation.

It was also recommended that a study be made of the ecology of water plants and the biological conditions of man-made water bodies, designed to reduce water losses through evaporation—a subject of great interest to hydrologists. Following this recommendation, Unesco made arrangements in 1970, with the help of the Freshwater Productivity Section of the IBP, for a study tour to be undertaken in South America in order to study the extent of spreads in South American inland waters, the biotic and environmental factors promoting their growth, and any existing biological agents for controlling species of *Salvinia* and *Eichhornia crassipes*. At the same time material was collected for the identification of these two species. The results of that study are described in *Ecology of Water Weeds in the Neotropics,* published by Unesco as Number 12 in the series *Technical Papers in Hydrology.*

The panel also recommended consideration be given to environmental management in relation to aquatic weed problems, to the preliminary ecological studies necessary prior to an intended change in the hydrological régime, and to research practices for obtaining an improved understanding of the ecology of water vegetation both under natural and experimental conditions and in different climatic regions. It was in order to fulfil this recommendation that Unesco arranged, again with the help of the Freshwater Productivity Section of the IBP, for the present publication to be written. This describes water weeds and the normal role of vegetation in water, as well as the ecology of excessive plant growth and its interferences in man's use of fresh water. Finally, it gives details of some specific programmes for the management of aquatic weed growth for the benefit of man, and possible control methods. This publication is mainly intended for the use of hydrologists, engineers and biologists dealing with infestations of aquatic plants, but it is hoped that it will also be of value

11

to a broader field of students, scientists and administrators interested in the techniques and consequences of environmental management.

Unesco acknowledges the valuable work done by the authors, Messrs J. J. Gaudet, T. O. Robson, R. D. Blackburn, F. D. Bennett, C. E. Boyd and particularly D. S. Mitchell who provided most of the material and undertook the editing of the publication.

Unesco is indebted to Dr J. Rzóska of the IBP for his advice and for his active collaboration in these projects.

For the most part, scientific names of plants have been used in the text. The sources of information have been omitted in the text, but may be found in the References, page 119. Common names have generally been avoided because of the wide differences between countries in this respect. All measurements are given in metric units; monetary values have been converted into United States dollars. Chemical formulae for herbicides may be found in the index of herbicides.

The authors wish to express their gratitude to the many scientists who provided them with information and assistance. Unfortunately limitations of time and space have made it necessary to restrict the treatment of certain topics to a minimum and, as a consequence, reference to much important work has not been possible. In particular it has proved impractical to include surveys of regional problems. The authors also grateful for the help received from Unesco and IBP.

1. Water weeds

D. S. Mitchell (United Kingdom)

1.1 INTRODUCTION

People concerned with the utilization of water and the management of water resources cannot fail to have been made aware of the problems that can be caused by the excessive growth of aquatic plants. The spread of Canadian pondweed, *Elodea canadensis,* through the canals and waterways of Western Europe during the latter half of the last century and, more recently, the colonization of large areas of tropical standing water by *Eichhornia crassipes* (Water Hyacinth) and *Salvinia molesta* (Kariba weed, African Pyle) exemplify the need for concern. Aquatic weed problems often follow man-made disturbances of the environment, both accidental and purposeful, and many of the problems caused by the three plants cited above and by other aquatic weeds occur out of the plants' natural distribution range following their introduction into alien areas. In the plants' native environments, troublesome growths are generally more likely to occur after environmental disturbance of the aquatic régime, such as by the construction of man-made lakes or artificial canals and waterways.

The widely used English epithet, 'water weeds', for plants growing in water gives one the firm impression that mankind generally regards aquatic plant growth as a nuisance. But is this always so? Are all aquatic plants weeds? Obviously there must be many exceptions and, at the outset, it is clearly important to consider the criteria that can be used to judge when an aquatic plant is a weed and when it is not. The word, or phrase, used for weeds in most languages implies that they are undesirable. English differs in employing a word to describe these plants that is intrinsically non-descriptive and the word 'weed' contrasts with words, or phrases, such as *Unkräuter, mauvaises herbes, malerbe, sornye rasteniya,* etc., which clearly imply that these plants are undesirable, or unwanted. King (1966) considered a number of definitions of weeds in general and concluded that there were ten characteristics which are commonly stated, or implied. These may be listed as : plants (1) growing where they are not wanted; (2) possessed of competitive and aggressive habits; (3) of wild and rank growth; (4) which were persistent and resistant to control or eradication; (5) consisting often of large populations with abundant, rank and extensive growths; (6) which were useless, unwanted, and undesirable; (7) which were harmful to man, animals, and crops; (8) exhibiting spontaneous growth, appearing without being sown or cultivated; (9) of high reproductive capacity; and, finally, (10) which were unsightly, disfiguring the landscape. Both in the choice of words used to describe weeds in most languages, and in the phrases employed to define them, it is clear that the definitions of these plants are mainly qualified by the degree to which they inhibit man's utilization or management of natural resources. This implies that a plant may be regarded as a weed in one situation and not in another. Thus characterization of a plant as a weed must involve subjective value-judgments which could lead to dispute. This is especially true of aquatic weeds, which, for our purposes, can be defined as *troublesome or unsightly plants growing in abundance in aquatic situations where they are not wanted.* This definition is not always easy to apply because water resources generally have more than one potential, if not actual, use for man and it follows that it is possible for a particular population of plants to interfere with one aspect of the utilization of a water body and to be beneficial for another, or to be a disadvantage in one part, such as a harbour, but no problem in another. In such cases, a careful evaluation of the various benefits of the water body is required before a wise decision can be made. Very often, however, a lack of knowledge about the structure and function of the ecosystem concerned makes this difficult. Nevertheless, it is important to attempt an evaluation of the part played by the supposed weed in the ecosystem, in so far as this can be established from general principles and from actual observation.

It is important to make a careful assessment of the situation in its broadest context before concluding that a particular population of plants constitutes a nuisance which warrants the application of control measures that are often expensive. Furthermore, it is also important to assess, as far as possible, the probable consequences of the control measures on the system. Man's history is already sufficiently full of errors of environmental manipulation.

1.2   THE IDENTIFICATION OF AQUATIC WEEDS

One of the first obstacles to be faced before a rational programme can be formulated to deal with an aquatic weed problem is the accurate identification of the plant, or plants, causing the difficulty. A useful first step is to establish which life form the plant in question habitually adopts. This is important, not only as an aid to identification, but also because different life forms have different responses to various environmental changes and therefore may demand different treatment. There are four main life forms which are related to the plant's position with respect to the water surface:
1. Free-floating plants.
2. Submerged plants generally attached to the bottom by roots.
3. Attached plants with floating leaves.
4. Surface plants with vegetative parts normally emerging above the surface of the water.

Some confusion may result in identifying the life form of attached plants after there has been a marked change in water level, as many aquatic plants are able to change their growth habit in response to different environmental conditions (Arber, 1920 ; Sculthorpe, 1967), and caution must be exercised at these times. It is also necessary to realize that many submerged and floating leaved plants have aerial inflorescences and flowers which emerge above the water. However, these difficulties are relatively minor and the establishment of the life form of an aquatic plant is generally a simple matter.

Determination of correct names for the plants in question has been much less straightforward, mainly because of the lack of comprehensive reference texts which could be readily used by the layman, though several important regional works are available (see Holm and Herberger, 1971). However, with the sponsorship of the

International Hydrological Decade, Cook (in preparation) is compiling an illustrated manual on the identification of aquatic plants and this will go a long way to alleviate this problem. If difficulty still exists, or there is doubt about the accuracy of determination, fully representative plant specimens should be sent to a competent herbarium for identification.

Aquatic plants are either adapted to continuous supplies of free water, or are at least tolerant of waterlogged soil conditions for substantial periods of time. The wide range of adaptation to varying amounts of water, and the impossibility of sharply distinguishing between aquatic and terrestrial environments, makes it difficult to define an aquatic plant precisely. Seasonal variation in the level of the water table and a plant's tolerance of this bring about a situation in which a plant may be growing with its lower parts submerged in water at one time of the year and, at other times, in a relatively dry substrate in exposed conditions. For the purposes of this manual, only the plants which habitually grow in running or standing free water will be considered. The same limitation would result if consideration was restricted to those plants growing in aquatic habitats, both natural (rivers, streams, lakes, ponds and swamps) and artificial (canals and man-made lakes). It is not proposed to deal with plants growing in marine situations and, for the most part, only vascular plants will be discussed. Phreatophytes (plants which grow in high water tables, such as along streams and river banks) will be referred to where appropriate but will not receive detailed treatment. Macroscopic aquatic plants are frequently termed aquatic macrophytes. This includes bryophytes (mosses and liverworts), which rarely cause difficulties, and large algae, which pose somewhat different problems demanding rather different treatment to vascular plants. In any case, most of the important aquatic weeds are all vascular plants and, for these, the more precise term, vascular hydrophytes, will be employed.

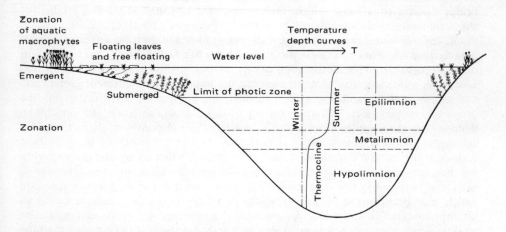

Figure 1. A diagramatic representation of a lake showing zonation of aquatic macrophytes, the photic zone and thermal stratification.

The adaptation of different life forms to different depths of water often results in a clearly marked zonation of aquatic vegetation from shore to deep water (Fig. 1). In a typical situation, the shallow water near the edge would be occupied by a zone of emergent species. As the water becomes deeper these are replaced by rooted forms with floating leaves, which in turn are fringed by a zone of submerged plants and/or free-floating species. The extent of each zone depends on the degree of change in depth and substrate. If follows too, that, in time, as organic matter accumulates on the bottom among the plants, there is a gradual decrease in depth as the water body ages. This will bring about a temporal succession of plants in which the zones replace one another as the water body is filled in. The species composition of each zone is dependent on many factors and depends on the environmental conditions and the ecological responses of the plants concerned.

The typical zonation and succession of aquatic macrophytes described above is modified in many ways. A lake shoreline exposed to wind and wave action will have a different type of zonation and species composition to one that is sheltered. The nature of the substrate will also have an effect. Similarly, zonation in a turbid water is likely to be different to that in a clear one. Conditions in a river also affect the composition of its aquatic plant communities and the vegetation in a stretch of a river will be affected by factors which are often interrelated, such as the rate of flow, the depth, the degree of turbulence, and the nature of the substrate. Thus, a plant community in a fast-running, stony section will be different to that where a meandering river is flowing slowly through muddy banks.

1.3   ENVIRONMENTAL REQUIREMENTS OF AQUATIC MACROPHYTES

Like other plants, aquatic macrophytes require nutrients and light to grow ; are affected by temperature, pH and type of substrate ; and are poisoned, or inhibited, by toxic substances and excessive amounts of certain environmental factors. While these factors modify the composition of the plant communities, they are in turn modified by the latter and the interaction between organisms and environment often brings about a situation in which 'the environment is almost as much a product of the community as the community is of the environment' (Westlake, 1959). Furthermore, environmental factors interact with one another and, in these circumstances, it is exceedingly difficult to analyse the effect of any one factor on any one component of the ecosystem. The recent applications of techniques of systems analysis and ecosystem modelling may assist to evaluate the importance of different factors and the nature of their ramifying effects through the ecosystem. Notwithstanding the present incomplete state of our knowledge of this complex situation, it is possible to deduce general principles which assist in understanding responses of plants to various factors in the environment. For convenience, the characteristics of each of these factors in the aquatic environment, and their general effect on aquatic macrophytes, will be considered separately. Only a very brief (and therefore superficial) resumé of each will be possible and it is essential to point out that the simplified impression which may be imparted by this approach could be dangerously inaccurate. In an attempt to offset this, the salient aspects of the structure and mode of function of aquatic ecosystems as a whole must also be briefly discussed at the conclusion of the chapter. The factors discussed are given more detailed treatment in a number of texts such as Welch (1952), Coker (1954), Hutchinson (1957, 1967), Liebmann (1960), Reid (1961), Ruttner (1963), Dussart (1966) and Hynes (1970). Also, for most purposes it is necessary to obtain as accurate a measurement as possible of these environmental parameters and textbooks, such as Welch (1948), Liebmann (1962), Mackereth (1963), Schwoerbel (1966), Strickland & Parsons (1965), American Public Health Association (1971) and Golterman & Clymo (1971) should be consulted for suitable methods.

1.3.1 Temperature

Ambient temperature depends upon climate and thus is affected by season, latitude and altitude, though thermal conditions in water are more equable than in the atmosphere and changes are slower. Plant metabolism depends upon temperature and is more rapid at higher temperatures. However, different species are adapted to different temperatures, some more narrowly than others, so that for each species there is an optimum temperature at which it functions best. Thus, changes in temperature can induce changes in species composition of plant communities by affecting the competitive ability of its components.

Temperature also has a number of indirect effects on aquatic plants through its effect on the behaviour of the system as a whole. In standing waters, surface heating in the summer is spread through the system by conduction as well as by wind- and wave-induced turbulence. The warmed upper layers become less dense and eventually sharply differentiated from the lower, colder, denser layers at a depth, which is determined by the interaction between the effectiveness of the water-mixing processes and the differences in density. At this depth, there is a comparatively rapid change in density, as indicated by a change in temperature, in a relatively narrow stratum of the lake. This part of the temperature depth curve is known as the thermocline and it separates the upper part of the lake, the epilimnion, from the lower hypolimnion (Fig. 1). The stability of this stratification depends on the persistence and extent of the temperature-induced density difference between the epilimnion and hypolimnion. The lake will remain stratified as long as the difference in density is sufficient to resist the water-mixing effect of the strongest storms. However, with the approach of winter, the water is cooled by the atmosphere until there is insufficient difference in density to maintain stratification and, at this time, a lake can be mixed by strong wind, the overturn resulting in isothermal conditions (Fig. 1). Lakes which become iced over will also exhibit an inverse thermal stratification in winter, mixing being induced by the spring thaw.

The rate of change of density with temperature increases as temperature increases, so that stable stratification can be established by smaller temperature changes in tropical than in temperate lakes. Furthermore, certain shallow bodies of water in the tropics are apparently stratified during the day and mixed at night. In others, overturn can be induced readily by cold rainfall, which induces relatively large increases in density, thus promoting active convection currents in the system. The formation of stable stratification also depends on the morphology of the lake basin, especially the relationship between surface area and depth. The stratification of lakes and their classification in terms of this is discussed in detail by Hutchinson (1957).

The effect of thermal stratification on vascular hydrophytes is mainly indirect through the promotion or inhibition of water mixing and the corresponding dispersion of nutrients and other chemical substances. The effects of these will be considered in a subsequent section.

Flowing bodies of water will obviously exhibit a different series of temperature changes. When flowing rapidly, there is considerable turbulence and thorough mixing so that temperatures are generally uniform. However, in reaches where the water is moving slowly, there may be some differentiation between surface and bottom waters. The initial temperature of the river or stream depends on its source and is therefore generally colder than air temperatures when supplied from melting snow or ice, while spring-fed streams may be warmer in winter and colder in summer. Temperatures in lower reaches usually reflect ambient air temperatures in that area and often approximate to the mean monthly air temperature at the place where the measurement is made. Diurnal variations may be considerable, especially in small bodies of water. Temperature alters the viscosity of water and, consequently, waters flow faster at higher temperatures and carry less silt. Hynes (1970) describes the thermal behaviour of flowing waters and should be consulted for more detail.

1.3.2 Light

Light is an essential requirement for photosynthesis and therefore for the growth of all aquatic plants. The depth to which submerged species can colonize the bottom of a body of water is thus dependent upon transmission of light through the water, though fluctuations in water level may allow plants to become established at depths beyond their normal range. Survival at these depths is possible, provided the photo-synthetic organs grow up into water where there is sufficient light for photo-synthesis.

The transmission of light is affected by the colour and turbidity of the water, the former affecting the composition of the transmitted light, and the latter the depth to which it penetrates. The effective photic zone is the layer of water within which there is sufficient light for photosynthesis to exceed respiration over twenty-four hours (Fig. 1). The depth at which light intensity is 1 per cent of the surface value is usually assumed to mark the limit of the photic zone. In clear waters, blue-green light penetrates further than light of other wavelengths, whereas, in brown waters, red and orange light penetrate furthest, though the photic zone is much smaller. Submerged plants are adapted to light of low intensity and this is often manifested in the morphology and physiology of the photosynthetic organs.

1.3.3 Dissolved gases

Submerged aquatic plants require dissolved carbon dioxide for photosynthesis and dissolved oxygen for respiration. Much less oxygen is available in water than in the atmosphere and a saturated solution of oxygen in water at 20° C will contain 9.2 mg/l at sea level. Solubility of oxygen increases with decrease in temperature and decreases with increase in altitude (decrease in atmospheric pressure). Diffusion of oxygen in water is very slow and, in calm water during ideal conditions for photosynthesis, supersaturated solutions of oxygen are likely to occur. For the same reason, water may rapidly become anoxic when a high demand for oxygen exists because of particular chemical or biological conditions.

The hypolimnia of certain lakes become anoxic during stratification and the rate at which deoxygenation occurs is more rapid in biologically productive lakes where biological oxygen demand is greater than in unproductive lakes, though Ruttner (1963) has pointed out that the higher metabolic rates in tropical waters will also increase the rate of deoxygenation.

Many vascular hydrophytes have adapted to the low oxygen tensions in water, particularly in bottom muds, by developing conducting air canals (aerenchyma).

Carbon dioxide is readily soluble in natural waters (about 200 times more than that of oxygen), its solubility also varying inversely with temperature and, in contrast with the atmosphere, the proportion of carbon dioxide to oxygen in water is nearly equal. In addition to its importance for photosynthesis, the chemical reaction of carbon dioxide with water and dissolved bases has a buffering effect on the water. Carbon dioxide reacts with water to form a weak acid which in turn reacts with the basal hydroxide to form bicarbonate or carbonate ions. The addition of acid or alkali results in a shift in the proportion of these forms of CO_2 rather than in a change in concentration of hydrogen ions and therefore of pH. The buffering effect is mani-fested best between pH 6 and 10 when HCO_3^- is the prevalent combined form of CO_2. Below pH 6, free CO_2 is more abundant, while, above pH 10, HCO_3^- is replaced by CO_3^{--}. The situation is a complex one and reference should be made to Hutchinson (1957), Gessner (1959), Reid (1961), Ruttner (1963) and King (1970), for detailed explanation.

The relationship between dissolved CO_2, pH and alkalinity in fresh water provides the most convenient method of measuring the CO_2 concentration. Alkalinity and pH must be accurately determined, the latter preferably by glass electrode, and the former by titration with standard acid to an end point of pH 4.5. At this pH, hydroxyl ions will have been removed, the equation below will have moved comple-tely to the right, and all bicarbonate will have been replaced by either dissolved CO_2 or undissociated H_2CO_3.

$$Base^+ + HCO_3^- + H_2O = Base^+ + H_2CO_3 + OH^-$$

Dissolved CO_2 present in a water sample can then be computed from a nomogram giving the relationship between this, pH and alkalinity (Mackereth, 1963).

Photosynthesis of plants utilizing free CO_2 and HCO_3^- upsets the equilibrium of the above equation and may increase pH of the waters in the photic zone.[1]

1.3.4 pH

The pH is the logarithm of the reciprocal of the hydrogen ion concentration and affects plant metabolism within the cell by affecting enzyme activity and, externally, by affecting the uptake of nutrients and carbon dioxide. Different species are adapted to different ranges of pH, and thus species composition in a water body may be altered by changes in pH. The pH of natural waters ranges from below 4.0 to above 10.0. Low values are found in lakes containing strong mineral acids such as certain volcanic lakes and bog pools. High pH readings are obtained from certain calcareous and alkaline lakes (Hutchinson, 1957).

1.3.5 Nutrient chemicals

Plant growth in fresh water is often limited by the availability of essential nutrients, at least during the active growing season. Waters which have an abundant supply of nutrients support larger plant populations, in which there is a rapid biological turnover. Such waters are consequently biologically highly productive and are said to be eutrophic. These may be contrasted with waters which are poor in nutrients and only poorly productive and which are termed oligotrophic. The high organic produc-tion of eutrophic waters results in a high oxygen demand so that eutrophic condi-tions are indicated by rapid deoxygenation of the hypolimnion following stratifica-tion.

In the higher temperatures of the tropics, nutrients are the factors most likely to limit growth and limitation by inorganic nitrogen appears to be the most widely manifested (Prowse & Talling, 1958; Nye & Greenland, 1960; Talling, 1965, 1966; Moss, 1969 ; Mitchell, 1970 ; Mitchell & Tur, in preparation ; Brinkman, personal communication), though sulphate (Beauchamp, 1953; Fish, 1956) and phosphorus

---

1. The ability of plants to obtain CO_2 for photosynthesis from HCO_3^- ions in the water has been a matter of some dispute but it appears that most algae and submerged vascular hydrophytes have this ability (Ruttner, 1963 ; Sculthorpe, 1967).

have also been suggested (Evans, 1961). In temperate fresh waters, phosphorus is considered by most workers to be the nutrient which most frequently limits primary productivity (Mackenthum, 1965; Thomas, 1969), though, in some cases, inorganic nitrogen is limiting (Malony, Miller & Blind, 1972) and in some soft waters, carbon also appears to be important (King, 1970; Martin, Bradford & Kennedy, 1970). The addition of the nutrient, or nutrients, limiting plant growth in a lake will result in its rapid eutrophication with consequent blooms of algae and luxuriant stands of aquatic plants.

Thermal stratification of a lake will also have an effect on the vertical distribution of nutrient chemicals within it. During the active growing period when the lake exhibits a summer stratification, nutrients are depleted from the epilimnion and accumulate in the hypolimnion from the decay of organic materials which fall into the latter. Furthermore, under anoxic conditions in the hypolimnion, certain ions such as PO_4^{---} and NH_4^- are released from the bottom muds (Mortimer, 1941, 1942). When the lake waters mix in winter or autumn overturn, many of these nutrients become available to organisms in the photic zone, though some are precipitated once again into the bottom muds under the oxygenated conditions which then prevail. This release of nutrients may result in a bloom of plant growth when other growth conditions are suitable. In tropical conditions, this bloom generally follows immediately after lake mixing.

Hutchinson (1969) has pointed out the importance of considering the lake, its bottom sediments and its catchment as a whole system which may be eutrophic, or oligotrophic, depending on the turnover time of the nutrients within it.

1.3.6   Toxic chemicals

The addition to water of chemicals that are toxic to plants is usually brought about by man. Pollution of fresh water by these and other means has recently received widespread publicity and most countries have introduced legislation aimed at controlling the quality of industrial and other effluents which it is permissible to discharge into fresh water.

1.3.7   Salinity

The salinity of natural waters has obvious effects on the composition of plant communities which occur in them. A few vascular hydrophytes are adapted to high salinities and occur in marine situations but, as stated earlier, it is not proposed to discuss these. Certain plants appear to tolerate considerable fluctuations in salinity and can therefore grow in estuarine or brackish conditions. These plants frequently have few competitors and may sometimes form extensive stands. However, most fresh water vascular hydrophytes are intolerant of increases in salinity for any length of time.

1.3.8   Substrate and turbulence

Permanent communities of aquatic plants, which are rooted in the bottom, are only established where the bottom is relatively stable. Certain species also show adaptation to either mud or sand/gravel substrates.

The turbulence of the water will obviously affect the size and distribution of the substrate particles and in this way will also affect plant communities. However, the turbulence also has a physical effect on the plants and will thus affect the appearance as well as the composition of these communities.

1.3.9   River and lake currents

The movement of water is more rapid in rivers than in lakes, though in both waters it is complex and readers are referred to texts such as Hynes (1970) and Hutchinson (1957). Water movement affects the pattern of distribution of sediment, is responsible for shaping the morphology of both river and lake, and determines the distribution and growth habit of vascular plant communities. In man-made lakes the inflow of comparatively large quantities of colder river water may result in a density current flowing at a certain level beneath the surface of the lake. This may have important consequences on the distribution of plant nutrients carried by the river water into the lake and thus on the growth of the aquatic plants.

1.3.10   River floods

The regular occurrence of floods in rivers which occur in regions with a markedly seasonal rainfall is probably the most potent factor affecting the nature and extent of vascular hydrophyte communities in these rivers and their flood plains. The rise in water level and the scouring action of the river flow usually have devastating effects on the aquatic plant populations in the main river channel. In addition, backwaters and pools on the river flood plain fill with flood water, and the consequent increase in depth and surface area loosens the floating plant communities. Therefore these are easily swept away by river currents, or blown by the wind against the shoreline, where they are often stranded when the water level drops after the floods and the surface area decreases again. The rise in water level may also have an adverse effect on attached aquatic plants but the extent of this effect depends on the depth to which the plants are submerged and the duration of the high flood level (Mitchell & Thomas, 1972).

1.3.11   The morphology of bodies of water

It has been shown that the limnological behaviour of a lake is determined to some extent by its morphology and it is obvious that the same must be true for rivers. This is particularly important in the design of man-made lakes and in the management of existing water bodies, because procedures can be based on predictions arising from measured parameters of the proposed or extant lake. Lake morphometry and its orientation to prevailing winds will affect not only the depth at which a thermocline becomes established, but also the degree of mixing of lake water, the nature of wind generated and density current movements, and the degree of shelter provided by coastline features for the growth of aquatic weeds.

1.3.12   Biotic factors

Any plant community is the result of the interaction of a number of biotic phenomena. Competition between species which are ecologically similar, grazing by animals, other animal utilization such as for nesting material, and the attack of pathogenic organisms will all affect the species composition and structure of plant communities. Aquatic plant communities are remarkable in that they are often dominated by one species and superficially appear to be monospecific in composition. Factors which lead to this situation are relatively little understood but the rapid rate of vegetative reproduction and/or the ability to take up and store nutrients (Boyd, 1969a) of which some species are capable is clearly important in some cases. These species quickly establish dominance over a suitable area so that potential competitors are prevented from becoming established. Such species often establish troublesome populations, especially on newly created waters.

Man's interference with aquatic ecosystems may have many effects depending on the type and extent of the interference. These range from the creation of new lakes and waterways to pollution and misguided management which may create conditions that are almost biologically sterile on the one hand, or undesirably over productive, on the other. While, strictly speaking, man is a biotic factor, his multifarious influences are so far-reaching and so different that it is often better to consider them separately as anthropogenic factors. The effects of some of these will become apparent from the content of succeeding chapters.

1.3.13 Aquatic ecosystems

The system of complex interrelationships which exists between living organisms and their non-living habitat is difficult to visualize and to delimit but ecologists have attempted to encompass this within the concept of an ecosystem. This is considered to comprise the spatially ordered, interrelated, dynamic organization of living communities and non-living environment, making up a recognizable part of the natural world system (the Biosphere). For example, a pond ecosystem, though not independent of its surroundings, may be said to consist of the plants and animals living in the aquatic environment provided by the pond and made up of its numerous physical and chemical parameters. The plant populations affect, and are affected by, the animal populations, both, in turn, affecting and being affected by different environmental factors.

Ecosystems are characterized by cycling systems in which chemical and biological processes ensure the circulation and re-use of natural resources in the system. Solar radiation is utilized to provide energy to maintain the existence of the system. In simple terms, photosynthesis by plants results in chemicals with high energy bonds (primary production). This energy is utilized in respiration to maintain the living processes of the plant cells, some being lost as heat, or is transferred to herbivorous animals consuming the plants. These animals, in turn, utilize some energy in respiration and pass some on to the carnivorous animals, which prey on the herbivores—and so on up the food chain. Dead material and detritus, which are derived from plants and animals not consumed in these food chains and from animal wastes, are utilized for energy by decomposer organisms and by detritus feeders. The acquisition of energy by heterotrophic organisms is considered as secondary production. Complex food webs exist in ecosystems, though a general principle which applies to all of these is that the total living mass (biomass) of primary producers is greater than that of the herbivores, which in turn is larger than that of the carnivores, and so on. Such a pyramid of biomass is an essential characteristic of a stable system. The same principles apply to the utilization of energy and a similar energy pyramid can be constructed (Phillipson, 1966). Recently considerable attention has been devoted to the study of the flow of energy through systems and readers are referred to the classic study of Odum (1957).

An important principle which is essential to an understanding of ecosystem structure and function is that there are no barriers limiting interactions between factors, i.e. the relationships are holocoenotic. Thus the effects of changes in any one factor can potentially ramify through the whole system. The complexity brought about by this characteristic is depicted in Figure 2.

Finally, stable ecosystems are homeostatic structures in which a built-in system of checks and balances provide a kind of dynamic stability. This property is dependent on the complexity of the system which allows alternative pathways when any one route is blocked. Man's interference with ecosystems frequently results in a reduction in species diversity with the consequent introduction of a potentially unmanageable instability.

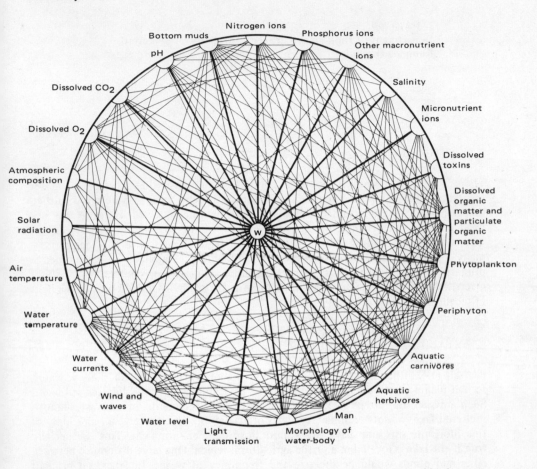

Figure 2. A diagramatic representation of the complex holocoenotic interrelationships between an aquatic weed (W) and various factors in its environment. The type of aquatic weed is not specified and only direct interactions are shown (after Billings, 1964).

2. The normal role of vegetation in water

J. J. Gaudet,
Department of Biological Sciences, University of Makerere,
Kampala (Uganda)

2.1 INTRODUCTION

There is a certain stability about a pond, lake or marsh that is often taken for granted. As pointed out in Chapter 1, it is not until such a natural system is disturbed that we begin to appreciate the regulatory mechanisms involved. Here we may ask what effect do plants have on the maintenance of this stability ? Or put another way, what is the normal role of vegetation in water ? In regard to macrophytes, many roles have recently been uncovered including : stabilization of sediments, primary production, detritus, nutrient uptake and release, competition, habitat diversification, and food source. All of these roles will be examined here in the light of recent work.

2.2 STABILIZATION OF SEDIMENTS

Pearsall (1921) has pointed out that along the margins of lakes in shallow water, rooted plants hasten the basin-filling process by trapping and consolidating sediment. Such aquatics are rare in rock-basin lakes with little sediments. In contrast, shallow, sheltered lakes on soft sedimentary rocks or glacial till, which receive a rich supply of fine inorganic silts and clays, are a more hospitable environment. This is especially true if the lake is located in a fertile agricultural region. One large difference between lakes and ponds would be the size and frequency of waves. In lakes, silt brought down by rivers will be swept away from the shore by wave action. The final destination of this silt will be determined by the rate of water movement and slope of the bottom. In a large lake the lake level will be raised close to the lake margin, and silt arriving subsequently will be deposited further out. Eventually, wave action will be prevented as: the basin fills, an increase in macrophytes occurs, and a pond habitat develops. This process differs considerably from lake to lake. In arid regions where the rate of silting is much slower, lakes when approaching extinction usually become so salty that vegetation is destroyed and a salt desert remains which is colonized by halophytes (Tutin, 1941).

Emergent aquatics seem to be the most efficient macrophytes at trapping silt from land run-off. Thus, reed swamps made up of emergent species are common in shallow basins or on river deltas where the basin-filling process is obviously in progress. But at the water edge and below the water surface in lakes and ponds, submerged and floating-leaved plants also intercept sediments. It has been shown by Pearsall (1921), and more recently by Spence (1967), that total plant cover in some lakes increases with decreasing particle size and increasing depth. Thus, fine silt particles form an ideal rooting medium for macrophytes. Once established, macrophytes trap even finer particles, and, in addition, will contribute much organic material from their own plant bodies. This results in a consolidated hydrosoil with varying organic content as illustrated in Table 1.

Table 1. Organic content of soil beneath ten different macrophyte communities (based on data of Pearsall, 1920)

Communities with characteristic plants	Organic content of soil (%)	
	Mean	Range
Submerged communities		
Potamogeton spp.	22.2	5-40
Myriophyllum spicatum	42.7	20-65
Juncus bulbosus form *fluitans*	86.6	60-96
Floating -leaved communities		
Nymphaea alba	25.7	10-35
Nymphaea alba var. *minor*	48.5	10-75
Potamogeton natans	74.2	60-92
Emergent communities		
Typha latifolia	34.0	20-50
Scirpus-Phragmites	44.7	20-65
Equisetum fluviatile	60.9	40-80
Carex spp.	89.4	80-95

Pearsall has shown that this increase in organic sediment is correlated with a decrease in influx of inorganic silt. Thus, macrophytes established on silted soils eventually are replaced by those capable of growth on organic soils.

The ability of macrophytes to trap sediments is not realized, however, unless they can become established. Shifting sediments or sediments of a highly organic nature delay their establishment. Thus, when suspended solids from sewage settle on a sandy or gravelly bed only certain macrophytes survive. A good example is the narrow-leaved pondweed, *Potamogeton pectinatus* (Butcher, 1933). This species does well since its long, smooth, narrow leaves are readily kept clear of settling particles or organisms. Other macrophytes will grow on such a substrate, but only when the suspended solids have been consolidated.

In rivers or streams the influx of organic matter from sewage effluents is often considerable. High rainfall increases this influx and results in water loaded with light particles which are difficult to trap. *Sphaerotilus,* the sewage 'fungus', may trap appreciable amounts, but particles not so trapped will be deposited only among the very fine muds and silts. The resultant loose organic substrate may be too mobile for rooted macrophytes. But if the substrate stabilizes, and the current slows, plant species adapted to individual niches will become established. These, in turn, will begin to alter the environment as they trap sediments along a river. From the data of Butcher (1933) it is possible to characterize different English riverine habitats and the sediments trapped as shown in Table 2.

Several factors are at work here, first, macrophytes slow the current velocity by their frictional resistance. Consequently particles come out of suspension, sometimes at a fast rate. The deposition continues to build on the downstream side and the macrophyte involved grows over the new material until an appreciable diversion has

Table 2. Relationship of macrophyte communities to current velocity, stream bed and sediment (based on data of Butcher, 1933)

Velocity of current	Nature of bed	Plant cover	Nature of community	Typical plants present	Sediments trapped
Fast.	Boulders.	Sparse.	Small cushions, tufts or crusts.	Algae, liverworts, mosses (*Fontinalis*).	Little or none.
Fast to moderate.	Stony.	Sparse (dense in chalk streams) with strong stems, small leaves.	Tough, woody rhizomes or roots forming a lattice-work.	Algae, mosses and *Myriophyllum spicatum, Potamogeton* spp., *Ranunculus fluitans*.	Silt and organic detritus.
Slow.	Sandy.	Sparse (dense in chalk streams) with fibrous roots or matted stems.	Plants which exhibit rapid growth, capable of quickly growing up through the covering layers of silt.	Algae and mosses are absent, replaced by *Callitriche stagnalis, and Sparganium emersum*.	Sand and silt.
Slow.	Silted.	Same as above.	Same as above.	Same as above, but, in addition, *Elodea canadensis*.	Mostly silt.
Negligible.	Muddy.	More or less plentiful.	Emergents with underground, fibrous roots or thick rhizomes.	Many of the above, but mostly *Glyceria aquatica*, or *Sparganium erectum*.	Silt and fine organic mud.

been built up (Hynes, 1970). Butcher, for example, recorded that a large clump of *Ranunculus fluitans* raised the level of a river bed by 17 cm over a five-month period. Macrophytes do not have to be rooted to cause particles to come out of suspension. Along calm stretches of 'white water' (characterized by its high load of sediment) on the Amazon River, floating meadows of aquatic grasses are common (Sioli, 1968). The roots of these floating macrophytes hang free under the mat and are often covered with a thick layer of fine sediments deposited from the 'white water'.

The second effect is the physical trapping of particles and consolidation of substrate. Thus, as Butcher pointed out, a sandy river bed covered with vegetation is not liable to undergo much shifting. Also, macrophytes rooted in shallow water protect river banks, or shores of lakes subjected to large changes in water level. When macrophytes are lacking, large quantities of sediment travel further downstream. A good example of this is given by Sioli (1968). On the Amazon River where 'white water' is too turbid to allow growth of submerged macrophytes, large amounts of sediment are not deposited until wide areas on the river are reached where islands of swamp forest impede flow.

A third, though less important, means of affecting sedimentation is the well-known phenomenon of marl deposition on the leaves of submerged aquatics such as

Potamogeton and *Chara*. This is in part caused by the removal of 'equilibrium' CO_2 from the water by the macrophytes, with a concomitant precipitation of carbonate salts. Wetzel (1960) found that submerged macrophytes (*Potamogeton, Najas* and *Myriophyllum*) in North American marl lakes develop considerable incrustations and this contributes to the inorganic sediments in these lakes.

During the final stages of silting up of a water body, reedswamps are usually present and if left unchecked will rapidly fill in large areas. This can be seen in Figure 3 where a *Glyceria maxima-Phragmites australia (P. communis)* reed swamp has almost occluded a series of bays and pools in a fen in Norfolk, England (Lambert, 1946). The amount of sediment trapped by such swamps and marshes in lower portions of river basins is quite large. Since the grass, *Spartina* x *townsendii*, first colonized the upper estuarine region of Poole Harbour in England in 1912, at least 1 million tons of sediment have been trapped by this marsh plant (Hubbard and Stebbings, 1968). In general, accretion (depth of sediment deposited per unit time) in temperate marshes averages 0.2 to 1.0 cm/year, but in *Spartina* x *townsendii* marshes in southern England, the rates (0.5 to 10.0 cm/year) are much higher (Ranwell, 1964). This resulted in 135 cm of silt in one marsh (Bridgwater Bay) being built up since *Spartina* was introduced to the area thirty-three years previously. Ranwell (1964) found such accretion to be positively correlated with the height of the marsh above reference, and the height and dry weight of *Spartina* stems. Thus *S. townsendii* stems in a different site (Poole Harbour) were much shorter than those in Bridgwater Bay and, consequently, the rate of accretion was only 0.5 to 1.0 cm/year (compared to 8 to 10 cm/year for Bridgwater Bay). About 40,000 m^3 of silt are estimated to be trapped at Bridgwater Bay annually, i.e. about 500 m^3/ha.year. With these rates in mind one can easily see that the amount of sediments trapped by macrophytes each year in these English marshes must be quite appreciable. One must also consider the large expanses of temperate marshland in northern Europe, the marshes along the eastern coast of North America, and in Eastern Europe ; the tropical swamps in the basins of large rivers such as the Nile, Niger, Congo, Amazon, Paraguay, and Ganges ; the extensive reed swamps of Okavango, Lukanga, Bangweulu, Upemba and Chad in Africa, the Grand Lac system in the Khmer Republic, and Gran Chaco in South America, Tasak Bera in Malaysia, the Rann of Kutch in south-eastern Asia, and the extensive swamps in southern Iraq, to mention some of the more important sediment 'sinks' in the world. In short, the trapping and stabilization of sediments by macrophytes is surely a most important factor in world-wide erosion patterns.

2.3 PRIMARY PRODUCTION

Sculthorpe (1967) has discussed at some length the mistaken notion that luxuriant submerged or floating macrophytes are unusually productive. There is now adequate proof that such plants are not very productive in comparison to other plant communities. The visual impression gained from observing the rapid spread of some notorious weeds is one of rapid growth. This is in itself correct since floating macrophytes often increase rapidly in areal cover. But such vegetation is necessarily buoyant and contains very little dry matter (see Table 3).

Thus the dry weight/unit area (biomass) for submerged and floating macrophytes will be low in comparison to communities such as a marsh or reed swamp. This

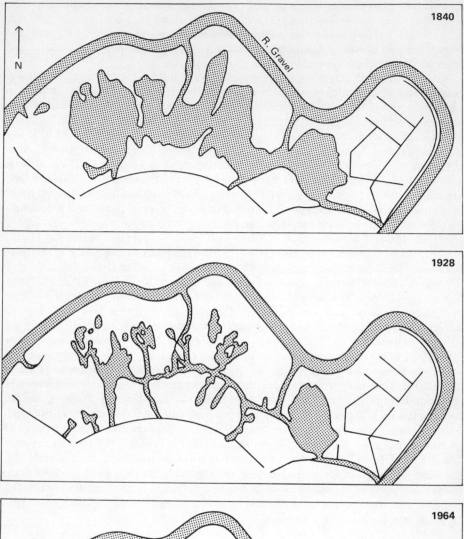

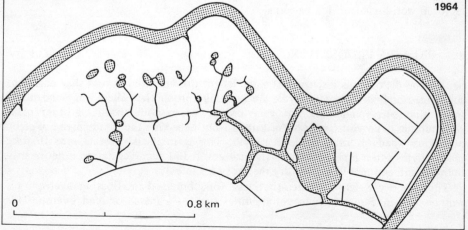

Table 3. Dry matter in various macrophytes (from Westlake, 1965)

Species type	Dry matter (percentage fresh weight)
Submerged species	
Myriophyllum alterniflorum	6
Ranunculus aquatilis	8
Hippuris vulgaris	11
Groenlandia densa	13
Floating or floating-leaved species	
Eichhornia crassipes	6
Callitriche stagnalis	7-9
Nasturtium officinale	5

comes about because emergent macrophytes contain much more dry matter (25 to 40 per cent, Sculthorpe, 1967). Because of this difference in dry-weight biomass (see Table 4), reed swamp or marsh emergents will be more productive, i.e. they will have higher annual rates of dry-matter production (Table 4).

Table 4. Estimates of biomass and production (based on a review by Westlake, 1963 and data from Thompson, 1972

Climate	Community	Dominant species	Dry - weight biomass (kg/m^2)	Annual mean production (t/ha.yr)	
				Dry weight	Organic
Temperate	Submerged in lake	*Ceratophyllum demersum*	0.71	9.0	7.1
Temperate	Submerged in river	*Berula erecta* and *Ranunculus penicillatus*	0.5	8.5	6.3
Subtropical	Submerged in spring	*Sagittaria eatonii* form *lorata* (and epiphytes)	0.81	27	21
Tropical	Floating	*Eichhornia crassipes*	1.5	15 to 44	11 to 33
Temperate	Marsh	*Typha* (hybrid)	4.6	⁻25	23
Tropical	Reed swamp	*Cyperus papyrus*	2.7 to 4.6	84 to 106	—

In order to compare the rates of production of macrophytes to that of other life forms it is necessary to take into account the inorganic component (i.e. ash) of dry matter produced. This is especially important for submerged macrophytes in marl lakes where heavy incrustations will also contribute to the ash content of samples. Data presented in Sculthorpe (1967) show submerged macrophyte communities contain, on the average, 21.3 per cent ash on a dry weight basis. Floating and emergent communities average much less, 11.5 per cent. In Table 4 dry weight production data corrected by Westlake for ash content give an estimate of organic production. Such estimates were then used to obtain probable annual average organic production (Westlake, 1963) and some of these are presented in Table 5 for comparison.

Figure 3. Progressive decrease in open water in an English fen (after Lambert, 1946, and Buttery & Lambert, 1965; reproduced by courtesy of the authors and the British Ecological Society).

Table 5. Probable annual average net primary productivity on fertile sites (from Westlake, 1963)

Type of ecosystem	Approximate organic productivity (t/ha.yr)	Range (± %)
Arid desert	1	50
Temperate lake phytoplankton	2	50
Temperate polluted lake phytoplankton	6	50
Temperate submerged macrophytes	6	20
Tropical submerged macrophytes	17	25
Temperate agriculture— annuals	22	15
Tropical agriculture— annuals	30	20
Tropical agri—peren— nials or reed swamps	75	15

It is obvious from these estimates that submerged aquatic macrophytes are among the poorest primary producers. The reverse is true for reed swamps which are among the highest.

Although submerged macrophytes are poor producers compared to other life forms, they may be quite important in an individual river, pond or lake. The work of Wetzel (1964) has pointed out their importance in one large, shallow, alkaline lake in California, and Table 6 summarizes his data. Here is the evidence that the macrophyte productivity on a year-round basis is not rapid, but it is quite fast during the growing season (seventy-five days). In fact it is faster than phytoplankton production during this season, and approaches one half the rate of periphyton (algae growing on the bottom mud surface). It would seem then, that primary production by submerged macrophytes may be significant in some lakes, especially when these are shallow.

Table 6. A summary of the primary productivity of Borax Lake, California (from Wetzel,1964)

Component	Annual mean (mgC/m^2.day)	Range (mgC/m^2.day)
Phytoplankton	249.3	10.4–524.5
Periphyton	731.5	0.0–5,760.0
Macrophytes during growing season only	372.3	0.0–982.2
Macrophytes on a year—round basis	76.5	0.0–982.2

2.4 DETRITUS

In general, the importance of the organic matter produced by macrophytes may lie in its eventual use as detritus, not as a direct food source. A large portion of the synthesized material produced by emergent macrophytes is contained in thick cellulosic cell walls. This sort of tissue is present, but in smaller quantities, in submerged macrophytes. As Russell-Hunter (1970) points out, most aquatic herbivores cannot use such tissue directly as food. Consequently, the decay and recycling of emergent vegetation is slower than for most macrophytes. In *Spartina* marshes on the south-eastern coast of North America the only herbivore capable of eating *Spartina* is the grasshopper, *Orchellimum fidicinium.* It consumes less than 1 per cent of the annual net production, consequently, the largest portion is left for bacterial decomposition (Smalley, 1960). As bacterial decomposition goes on, amino acids and B_{12} vitamins are released, and these in turn are used by marsh animals for growth (Starr, Jones & Martinez, 1957). The vitamins released from bacteria growing on *Spartina* detritus step up protein production by other organisms and, in this way, 11 per cent of the *Spartina* is eventually converted to animal protein.

The most important aspect of macrophyte detritus cycling seems to be time. Time is required for release of molecules small enough to be taken up by other steps in the food web. A very slow cycling is typical of sulphur from macrophyte detritus deposited in the aerobic bottom muds in shallow portions of Lake Victoria (Hesse, 1957, 1958). This sulphur is deposited after initial breakdown of the detritus and represents 0.3 to 1.0 per cent of the dry weight of the mud. It is primarily in an organic form. This organic sulphur is present even at depths of 10 to 15 m where it has remained for several thousands of years. The plants responsible are the submerged, floating and emergent vegetation common to the lake edge. This sulphur 'trap' is said to be the cause of low sulphur in the water of this lake (the second largest in the world) and has been cited as one of the possible factors limiting production there (Beauchamp, 1953).

The amount of carbon trapped in the sediments in some lakes can be quite large. In the sediments of Lawrence Lake, Michigan, Rich (1970) found 2×10^6 g organic carbon/m^2. This has been produced at the rate of 14.8 g/m^2 year over the *c.* 14,000 years of the lake's existence. Macrophytes are responsible for about 60 per cent of the lake's carbon input and would be the major contributor to the carbon in the upper 8 cm of sediment which is involved in the detritus cycle in this lake. The uncycled carbon remains trapped in the permanent sediments.

A much faster cycling of carbon occurs when macrophytes excrete dissolved organic compounds directly. Wetzel (1969) felt it likely that macrophytically released dissolved organic compounds are taken up quickly by periphyton, such as sessile algae and bacteria, growing on a macrophyte. Such compounds would tend to be utilized without even entering the aquatic milieu. Wetzel & Manny (1971) found 5 to 25 per cent of the photosynthetic carbon fixed was excreted by the submerged aquatic, *Najas flexilis,* in axenic culture. A much lower percentage was released by the floating macrophyte, *Lemna perpusilla.*

Thus, even before death and degradation, macrophytes contribute organic matter which, according to Wetzel & Manny, can significantly influence nutrient cycling and secondary production rates of the pelagic zone.

2.5 NUTRIENT UPTAKE

In addition to organic matter from the detritus cycle, macrophytes contribute organic and inorganic nutrients to the aquatic ecosystem. This is part of the natural cycle, since rooted aquatic plants have access to mineral nutrients which are often not available to non-rooted macrophytes or phytoplankton. In shallow areas populated by macrophytes the aerobic sediments prevent the release of nutrients such as phosphorus from the deeper anaerobic mud. And as Boyd (1967) points out '. . . penetration of roots into anaerobic layers probably allows for the uptake of quantities of nutrients in excess of the amounts that would otherwise reach the water for foliar absorption'.

The best-known examples of nutrients being taken up by these plants are given by the reed-swamp emergents such as *Spartina, Phragmites* and *Typha.* Most of the sites studied have been in temperate regions but, more recently, investigations have been undertaken of reed swamps in tropical regions, such as the *Typha* swamps of Lake Chilwa in Malawi (Howard-Williams, Furse, Schulten-Senden, Bourn & Lenton, 1972) and the papyrus swamps of East Africa in the upper portion of the Nile Basin (Thompson & Gaudet, in press). Some of the most extensive original studies on nutrient uptake by emergent macrophytes have been done by Boyd (1969*a*, 1970*a*) and Boyd & Hess (1970). These last authors found that standing crop (dry-weight biomass) of *Typha latifolia* was strongly correlated with the phosphorus content of the hydrosoil (dilute acid soluble), and the water standing above the hydrosoil. They also found significant (but not strong) correlations between environmental levels of several nutrients and tissue levels in this plant. The levels of these nutrients within *Typha* rose faster than the standing crop, since Boyd (1970*a*) obtained considerably more than 50 per cent of the net mineral accumulation before 50 per cent of the maximum dry-matter crop was produced. The standing crop for mature (flowering) plants varied between 428 and 2,252 g dry matter/m^2. The average concentration of various nutrients as percentages of dry weight in *Typha latifolia* (Boyd & Hess, 1970) is shown in Table 7.

Table 7. Concentration of various constituents as percentages of dry weight in *Typha latifolia* (from Boyd & Hess, 1970) compared to a mean for eleven emergent, floating and submerged macrophytes (based on Boyd, 1967).

	Ash	Carbon	N	P	Ca	Mg	K	Na	S
Typha	6.75	45.91	1.37	0.21	0.89	0.16	2.38	0.38	0.13
Mean for Macrophytes	17.12		2.69	0.27	2.02	0.52	3.27	0.62	

The more useful way of expressing the amount of each nutrient taken up by such macrophytes is shown in Table 8. Here standing crops and their percentage composition were used to compute the quantity of nutrients present in the plant. Since there is a large variation in standing crop of macrophytes such as *Typha* (see below) it may '. . . be hazardous to predict levels of chemical constituents in a particular aquatic plant community from existing data' (Boyd, 1970*b*). But, it does not require much reflection to realize that the removal of such levels of nutrients from sediments must be a considerable factor in the ecology of shallow water communities. This would be especially true of the delicate rooted submerged macrophytes such as *Myriophyllum* which will decompose at a faster rate than the more resistant emergent species.

This tendency towards accumulation of mineral nutrients by aquatics has some important side-effects. Ophel & Fraser (1970) observed that '. . . organisms utilize strontium less effectively than calcium—that is, they discriminate against strontium in favour of calcium'. Some macrophytes, however, have the reverse effect, and thus act as a concentration step in aquatic food webs. Ophel & Fraser investigated

Table 8. Standing crops (g dry wt/m^2) of several macrophytes and the content of various constituents in that standing crop (compiled from Boyd, 1967, 1969a, 1970a, 1970c)

Species type	Standing crop	Ash	N	P	Ca	Mg	K	Na	S
Emergent species									
Typha latifolia	684	33.53	3.49	0.77	3.87	0.76	14.17	1.64	0.62
Schoenplectus (Scirpus) americanus	150	11.80	1.74	0.23	0.97	0.45	2.59	0.34	0.99
Justicia americana	2,458	377.79	42.03	2.78	17.94	14.99	75.22	–	3.98
Alternanthera philoxeroides	841	123.80	24.14	2.69	4.37	4.37	43.73		2.44
Floating species									
Eichhornia crassipes	1,280	230.40	20.48	5.50	12.80	14.08	55.04	4.35	4.22
Submerged species									
Myriophyllum	222	30.60	9.20	0.93	5.06	1.64	4.10	–	0.95
Ceratophyllum	666	148.40	16.60	1.33	17.33	7.33	–	–	1.20
Chara	1,120	482.33	27.33	2.77	89.22	10.22	26.11	–	6.11

twenty-two macrophytes species from various communities in Perch Lake in Ontario and found only four species which did not discriminate against calcium in favour of strontium.

In general, macrophytes would provide an enrichment step for strontium relative to calcium. As Ophel & Fraser point out, this role of aquatic plants has far-reaching effects on herbivorous fish, which in Perch Lake are known to have strontium : calcium ratios almost three times greater than carnivorous fish.

The adverse effects of ^{90}Sr from radioactive fall-out on humans is too well known to dwell on here and the role of macrophytes in the cycling of this element must not be underestimated.

2.6 NUTRIENT RELEASE

As pointed out in the section on detritus, the organic components of a given macrophyte may be recycled very slowly or very quickly depending on environmental conditions and whether decomposition is involved. Boyd (1970d), for example, analysed leaves of *Typha latifolia* from fibre-glass bags which had been anchored in a swamp on the surface of the mud beneath 30 cm of water. He found that most mineral nutrients were rapidly lost from the plant. After 20 days only 5 per cent K and 7 per cent Na remained from the original 100 per cent. After 200 days only 10 per cent Mg, 25 per cent Ca, 50 per cent P and 60 per cent N remained.

In addition to nutrients released during decomposition, emergents also contribute nutrients very quickly from their litter by elution. Planter (1970) found maximum levels of soluble nutrients from air-dried pieces of stem and leaves of *Phragmites australia (P. communis)*, eluted into lake water after only twenty-four hours. Increases above normal lake water level calculated from his data appear as follows : Na 27 per cent, K 54 per cent, P 88 per cent, N as ammonia 89 per cent. Ca did not increase (–16 per cent) until carbonated water was used, then it eluted rapidly. Aquatic macrophytes release such minerals much faster than terrestrial plants, and are capable of shortening the mineral regeneration time considerably.

2.7 COMPETITION

In Table 8 it can be seen that non-rooted plants, such as *Ceratophyllum* and the floating macrophyte *Eichhornia*, contain significant quantities of various nutrients. Unlike emergents these plants absorb the bulk of their nutrients from the water above the hydrosoil. Such macrophytes are, therefore, in direct competition for dissolved nutrients with other plants, especially the phytoplankton, and periphyton (the algal layers on rocks, mud, etc., also referred to as Aufwuchs).

Submerged macrophytes will succumb to large increases in phytoplankton because of the shading effect. Such large increases in phytoplankton can be caused by sudden large increases in nutrients, e.g. by fertilization (Mulligan & Baranowski, 1969) or by an influx of sewage (Hynes, 1960). On the other hand, floating macrophytes respond to such large increases in nutrients by growing to cover an increased area, thus shading out phytoplankton and all other macrophytes except emergents.

Emergent macrophytes are markedly exclusive, since they often occur in dense monospecific stands reminiscent of monocultures. Boyd (1969*a*) suggested that this comes about because of their success in taking up and storing nutrients which are later made available to young growing organs by translocation. During the peak growing season, the growth of emergents is not limited, but nutrients are no longer available for competitors. Other factors such as light and toxins are also involved. In equatorial papyrus swamps the growth season is continuous, nutrients are plentiful, and yet papyrus has very little competition because it shades out most other emergents (Beadle & Lind, 1960).

2.8 HABITAT DIVERSIFICATION

There is no doubt that the appearance of macrophytes in aquatic ecosystems leads to an increase in the number of other plants and animal species/unit area. English river beds consisting of stones and gravel support $3\text{-}4 . 10^3$ invertebrates/m^2, while those beds covered with aquatic mosses or other weeds support $6\text{-}40 . 10^4$/m^2 (Percival & Whitehead, 1929 ; Westlake *et al.*, 1972). In addition, sessile algae, especially diatoms, abound. Thus macrophytes, in addition to and as a consequence of the chemical and physical changes they induce in the aquatic environment, bring into being a much more diversified habitat for animals and plants.

Chemical changes in relation to cycling of dissolved organic compounds from macrophytes, which possibly are a direct source of food for periphyton (Aufwuchs) have already been mentioned. Another chemical factor in the establishment of the faunas of macrophytic microhabitats would be the daily rate of oxygen production. Sculthorpe (1967) has suggested that vigorous oxygen production may benefit the aquatic fauna whenever temperatures are high and oxygen is scarce. The amount of oxygen produced by macrophytes during daylight hours will vary considerably depending on the average net production of the particular community. Macrophytes in English rivers, estimated from the crop data of several workers, may produce 0.13 to 7.36 g oxygen/m^2 per day as an average rate over long periods. Around noon on fine days, rates of the order 1 g oxygen/m^2 . hr are likely (Sculthorpe, 1967).

Once microhabitats are established, the surface of most macrophytes is quickly colonized by organisms. Colonization of long strap-shaped leaves of *Sagittaria*, for example, begins while the young leaf is quite small (Odum, 1957). In 26 days, because of linear expansion at the leaf base, the colonized region is pushed up to the top of the plant where it is then easily grazed on by small and large organisms alike. In a *Sagittaria eatonii (S. lorata)* community, 1 m^2 of bottom mud will support 24.3 m^2 of *Sagittaria* leaf surface, of which about 6 m^2 is covered with Aufwuchs. This area of Aufwuchs contains approximately: 1.5×10^{12} bacteria; 2.4×10^{11} algal cells; 2.1×10^5 midge larvae; and 6×10^4 caddis-fly larvae. These organisms are firmly attached and must be scraped off. There are a number of other organisms, such as copepods, mites, gammarids, etc., which are included in the fauna of a *Sagittaria* leaf. The standing crops of such populations are of considerable importance to fish production.

Macrophytes physically change aquatic ecosystems in several ways which are important in habitat diversification. They slow down the movement of stones in fast stretches of river (Butcher, 1933). Consequently, the number of species increases in previously unproductive regions. The mesh formed by finely divided leaves of some submerged species (e.g. *Myriophyllum*), or the network of filaments formed by some algae (e.g. *Hydrodictyon,* or *Nitella*), provides excellent refuge for young or small animals. These are also ideal sites for egg-laying by certain fish and after egg hatching they also serve as a nursery. Several insect larvae, e.g. caddis-flies, and fish, e.g. sticklebacks, use submerged macrophyte material in the construction of nests. The older rhizomes of reed-swamp emergents such as papyrus or any soft woody material present in shallow water provide a burrowing substrate for several burrowing insects, such as the mayfly, *Povilla adusta.* This invertebrate is a most important link in the food web of natural (e.g. Lake Victoria) and man-made tropical lakes (e.g. Volta Lake). In these lakes it is a consumer of phytoplankton and periphyton and, in turn, is an important food for many fish species (Petr, 1970). Emergent plants also provide the rather special conditions needed by swamp inhabitants, such as the swamp worm, *Alma emini.* In papyrus swamps in the Nile River basin, *Alma* is commonly present in the upper 60 cm of the papyrus mat (Beadle & Lind, 1960). This worm is adapted to life under anaerobic conditions and can even live for several days without oxygen. In such swamps, *Alma* digests large amounts of detritus.

Emergent macrophytes often provide extensive areas of plant cover above water. This provides nesting material and nesting sites for a large number of small birds, insects, and spiders. In papyrus swamps, each papyrus stem is terminated by a large umbel with many long rays. Thornton (1957) found each umbel supported a fauna which was strongly correlated with umbel development. The early animal populations on young umbels are isolated until the umbel rays are long enough so that the umbels begin to contact one another. Populations of predators develop at this time, and then emigrate to other umbels. Another emergent, *Phragmites australis,* serves as a host for the parasitic smut fungus, *Ustilago grandis,* in addition to other plant and animal pests (Durska, 1970). Thus, emergents allow for the development of very intricate food webs in their aerial portions.

Floating macrophytes are now known to cause considerable changes in the fauna associated with plants in shallow water regions. It seems submerged plants, such as *Ceratophyllum,* tend to support a large fauna (7,920 individuals) consisting of filter feeders and browsers (Petr, 1968). On the other hand *Pistia*, a free-floating, rosette-forming macrophyte has a smaller fauna (4,314 individuals) consisting mostly of predators. One would expect the above results, since floating macrophytes tend to shade out phytoplankton and submerged macrophytes, resulting in an environment which is not acceptable to herbivorous species. Likewise, in another man-made African lake, Lake Kariba, McLachlan (1969) reported that the appearance of submerged macrophytes, such as *Potamogeton* and emergents, such as *Ludwigia,* have resulted in marked changes in the benthic fauna. Mud species increased from 28 to 46 in the bottom mud close to the base of these plants. This change involved the appearance of 21 species new to the area, and a disappearance of 3 species. The floating macrophyte, *Salvinia,* however, caused a large depression of mud fauna ; all species save one disappeared from the mud beneath the mats which formed. *Salvinia* did support a large predator population (10 species) in the dissected leaf mass which hangs down under the floating leaves. Again, these are results which seem correlated with the shading effects of floating macrophytes.

Macrophytes bring about changes which slowly and inexorably lead from an aquatic to a terrestrial existence. During this transition many organisms are affected, including the macrophytes themselves. One can see this reflected in the nutrition of species growing in the new habitat. For example, as one moves away from a lake into a swamp or bog, the nitrogen content in the soil decreases (Table 9). Consequently, only macrophytes adapted to a low nitrogen environment will survive.

Table 9. Comparison of average nitrogen contents of plants and soil from several different sites (based on Gorham, 1953)

Site	Nitrogen (%)	
	Soil	Plant
Lakes	4.13	4.63
Reed swamps	3.13	2.53
Bogs	1.89	1.63

2.9 FOOD SOURCE

Herbivorous fishes, such as *Tilapia rendalli* and *Ctenopharyngodon idella,* will feed on aquatic plants. Though there is some indication of preference for submerged plants (e.g. Elodea, Ceratophyllum and Najas), floating plants (e.g. duckweeds) and emergent plants (e.g. Typha, Glyceria) are also eaten (Sculthorpe, 1967; Blackburn, Sutton & Taylor, 1971). In regard to the large algae, intact cellulose walls are not digested, thus, *Oedogonium,* where the cell caps break open easily, is more digestible than the stronger filaments of *Spirogyra* (Prowse, 1964). As indicated earlier, the periphyton growing on the surface of macrophytes is also quite important as fish food.

In streams and rivers many macrophytes are apparently unpalatable to invertebrates (Hynes, 1970). Aquatic mosses seem to be an exception, since these are eaten by a range of arthropods, often in large amounts. This also seems true for crayfish in deep lakes where aquatic mosses abound (Franz & Cordone, 1967). Crayfish in shallow lakes, however, feed on a variety of submerged macrophytes such as *Potamogeton, Ceratophyllum, Elodea, Myriophyllum, Chara,* and *Vallisneria* (Dean, 1969). In shallow portions of lakes certain insects consume significant amounts of macrophytes. Smirnov (1961) found the beetle, *Galerucella nymphaeae,* consumed 224 per cent of its own weight in *Nymphaea candida* leaves daily. This food contained very little fat and Smirnov suggested that the insect was probably extracting protein from the cell contents and passing out the excess cellulose. He rated several beetles using a daily food index based on the mean ratio of the weight of the food eaten to the weight of the consumer. His results are shown in Table 10. Gajevskaya (1966) has discussed the role of aquatic plants in the nutrition of the

Table 10. Daily food index of several beetles feeding on macrophytes (based on Smirnov, 1961)

Plant	Beetles	Daily food index (%)[1]
Sagittaria sagittifolia	*Donacia dentata*	3–22
Nymphaea candida	*Donacia crassipes*	8–54
Typha latifolia	*Donacia vulgaris*	29
Cicuta virosa	*Lixus iridis*	43
Cicuta virosa	*Phytonomus arundinis*	53–124
Lycopus europaeus	*Cassida viridis*	168
Sagittaria sagittifolia	*Hydronomus alismatis*	258

1. Daily food index is the mean ratio of the weight of the food eaten to the weight of the consumer, expressed as a percentage.

animals inhabiting fresh water environments and should be consulted for further details.

Macrophytes are a direct source of food for many wild animals. Fassett (1969) lists 210 species of North American macrophytes, various portions of which are eaten by about 72 species, including: 43 wildfowl, 14 marsh and shore birds, 10 upland game birds and 5 wild mammals. On a world-wide basis the number of wild bird species so supported must be very large.

The emergents at the water edge and in reed swamps are obviously very important as bird food. They comprise 60 per cent of the species in Fassett's list. Submerged species are also important for waterfowl. Lake Naivasha in Kenya supports 31,000 ducks (6 spp.) and 43,500 coot, *Fulica cristata* (Watson & Parker, 1970). The ducks forage on a wide range of aquatics, but the coots depend heavily on the submerged plant, *Najas pectinata* (Watson, Singh & Parker, 1970).

Lake Naivasha also supports a large population of coypu, *Myocastor coypus*, which enjoy the emergent vegetation around the lake edge. Coypu are also common in the Norfolk reed swamps in Britain where they feed on shoots and rhizomes of *Phragmites, Glyceria* and *Typha* (Lambert, 1946). Other mammals in certain regions will graze on macrophytes. These include cattle, pigs, goats, sheep, beaver, deer, moose, porcupine, musk-rat, hippopotamus, manatee and dugong (Sculthorpe, 1967). As a source of human food, naturally occurring aquatics are generally unimportant. The cultivation of certain aquatics for food is, however, important and is discussed in Chapter 7.

3. The development of excessive populations of aquatic plants

D. S. Mitchell (United Kingdom)

3.1 INTRODUCTION

A number of vascular hydrophyte species are notorious for their spectacular capacity for explosive population growth. Other species are particularly well adapted to certain environmental conditions and, over a period of time, establish large populations of almost pure stands of the same species. While the conditions which gave rise to this situation remain, these plant species are likely to maintain large standing crops which would be difficult to eliminate or to replace with vegetation that may be considered more desirable. This situation is most frequently encountered in swamps and extensive stands of *Phragmites* spp., *Typha* spp. and *Cyperus papyrus,* among others, are conspicuous features in many regions of the world.

In general, the factors which contribute to the development of these excessive populations of aquatic plants can be attributed to two sources: the existence of particular ecological conditions and the adaptation of certain plant species to take advantage of these conditions. Initially, it is convenient to distinguish between those plant species with a marked capacity for rapid multiplication of individuals (generally floating) and those which exhibit tenacious growth within certain, fairly narrow, ecological limits (generally rooted), though some of the latter species are capable of rapid colonization of an area.

3.2 FLOATING OR GENERALLY NON-ROOTED AQUATIC WEEDS

The aquatic weeds that cause some of the most widespread and serious problems fall into this group. *Eichhornia crassipes, Salvinia molesta* and *Azolla* spp. all have a free floating life-form, while *Ceratophyllum demersum* is characteristically unattached and may form large masses drifting about just below the surface of the water. Members of this group of species are generally characterized by a number of factors which undoubtedly contribute to their success. Those that appear to be most important are: a capacity for rapid vegetative multiplication; an ability to regenerate from relatively small portions of vegetative thallus; a complete or partial independence from the strictures of sexual reproduction, which, even if manifested, seldom seems to play a major part in the establishment of excessively large populations; a growth morphology, which results in a large area of photosynthetic tissue in proportion to the whole plant body that rapidly occupies the available water surface or photic zone; and finally, an independence of substrate conditions and fluctuations in water level. Because they are unattached, populations of these plants are seldom permanent and, if space permits, are liable to be moved by wind and water currents or, if confined in one place, initiate the accumulation of organic matter which decreases the depth of the body of water until it is sufficiently shallow for the establishment of emergent swamp vegetation. Thus they are essentially primary colonizers in aquatic ecosystems.

3.3   ATTACHED SUBMERGED AND EMERGENT WEEDS

Attached aquatic plants are usually dependent for good growth on a stable hydrological régime and are generally less likely to be a problem in situations where rapid or extensive fluctuations in water level occur, though they may be tolerant of short-term changes. Submerged species can only grow where there is sufficient light and may be adversely affected by the onset of factors such as turbidity and excessive populations of planktonic algae, which decrease the penetration of light into the water. From this, it is clear that these species are restricted to specific environmental conditions, but because they are particularly well adapted to these conditions they tend to occupy the available area almost completely and will rapidly colonize new areas if the required conditions are established in them.

Specialized communities of emergent species may develop on a substratum of floating aquatic plants, especially when stands of these are particularly stable. These communities form floating islands, or sudd (Penfound & Earle, 1948; Boughey, 1963; Tur, 1965; Mitchell, 1969; Junk, 1970; Mitchell & Thomas, 1972) and can be very troublesome if they drift about on an open water surface.

3.4   RAPID VEGETATIVE GROWTH

At the basis of all examples of the explosive development of excessive populations of aquatic plants is the vegetative growth of the plants themselves. Thus it is desirable to examine briefly the phenomenon of plant growth and review techniques that have been used to measure this in aquatic plants.

3.4.1   Growth analysis

The growth of a plant depends on its ability to increase in size through increase in the number of cells and enlargement of new cells to full size. Two processes are therefore involved and both are ultimately dependent, to some extent, on the absorption of inorganic nutrients, and on the process of photosynthesis, in which the plant fixes carbon and hydrogen to form high energy carbonates. Growth is eventually limited by environmental or other factors. Thus if growth increments are plotted against time a sigmoid curve is obtained as the initial exponential gives way to equilibrium between growth and decay.

Exponential biological growth has been shown to be of the mathematical form:

$$X_t = X_o \cdot e^{Kg.t} \qquad (1)$$

or

$$\ln X_t = \ln X_o + Kg \cdot t \qquad (2)$$

where X_0 is the initial size, X_t is the size after period, t, and K_g is the rate of growth; $\ln = \log_e$. Growth of this type occurs when the material added contributes to the growth potential of the organism. Thus, the sizes of growth increments increase within equal time periods, as growth continues, and it is more realistic to calculate relative growth rate *(RGR)*, which is defined as the increase of material per unit of material present per unit of time, rather than growth rate *(GR)*, which is simply the increase of plant material per unit of time and does not take into account the quantity of material present. Relative growth rate can also be reported as percentage increase per day. The second expression (2) above is of the form $y = c + m.x$, where y is the dependent variable (X_t), x is the independent variable *(t)*, m is the slope (K_g) and c is the intercept on the Y axis (X_o). This implies that, while K_g is constant, the successive sizes of the organism, expressed as ln, should lie on a straight line when graphed against time, the slope of the line depending on the size of the growth factor, K_g. K_g may thus be readily determined by computing the regression between time and the dependent sizes of organisms and its constancy assessed by testing the significance of the regression with a *t*-test. Alternatively, it is clear from the first expression (1) that

$$K_g \text{ or } RGR = \frac{\ln X_t - \ln X_o}{t} . \tag{3}$$

Fisher (1920) has explained in detail the derivation of this formula to determine mean relative growth rate $(\overline{RGR})$ and Radford (1967) has pointed out that it is not necessary to assume exponential growth to use the formula to derive the mean relative growth rate during the period in question, t, because the value of $\overline{RGR}$ is given by (3) no matter how X and RGR change with time. However, if growth is exponential, then, not only is mean relative growth rate given by the formula (3), but it can also be said that the relative growth rate held this value throughout the whole period, t.

Growth, and therefore ultimately yield or standing crop, must depend on the level of photosynthesis per unit of leaf surface and the size of the assimilatory area. Since the ash fraction of the cells of the leaves of most plants is small and relatively constant, gain in dry weight is a measure of the excess of carbon dioxide fixed in photosynthesis over that respired in respiration. On this basis, another useful growth parameter, mean net assimilation rate, $\overline{NAR}$, can be calculated. This may be defined as the increase of plant material per unit of assimilatory material per unit of time and can be computed from the formula:

$$\overline{NAR} = \frac{W_2 - W_1}{A_2 - A_1} . \frac{(\ln A_2 - \ln A_1)}{(t_2 - t_1)} \tag{4}$$

where W_1 and A_1 are, respectively, dry weight and leaf area at time t_1 and W_2 and A_2 dry weight and leaf area at time t_2. This formula can only be applied if A and W are linearly related over the time period t_1 to t_2 and if A and W are not discontinuous functions of time. However, errors are only likely to be slight if measurements are made at intervals of less than two weeks. Plants with a high net assimilation rate are likely to form large populations in a relatively short period.

It is inappropriate to discuss the full mathematical bases of all the formulae referred to above and readers are referred to Fisher (1920), Williams (1946), Watson (1952), Blackman (1960), Radford (1967), Hammerton & Stone (1966), Sestak, Catsky & Jarvis (1971) or Evans (1972), for this and more detail on the history of the development of growth analysis formulae and their application.

3.4.2 Assessment of the growth and extent of aquatic plant populations

The methods of growth analysis described above were used by Mitchell (1970) and Mitchell & Tur (in preparation) to investigate the growth rate of *Salvinia molesta* in culture and in Lake Kariba, Central Africa, the results for relative growth rate being reported in terms of percentage per day.

Bock (1969) calculated a daily increment factor (X) for *Eichhornia crassipes* from the formula :

$$N_t = N_o \cdot X^T \tag{5}$$

where N_o is the initial number of plants, N_t is the final number of plants and T is the time interval in days. It can be seen that this formula is similar to formula (2) and

$$X = e^{K_g} \tag{6}$$

Thus $\ln X = K_g = \overline{RGR}$ and Bock's daily increment factor can be converted to a mean relative growth rate by taking out its logarithm to the base e (natural logarithm).

Growth of aquatic weeds has also been reported in terms of doubling time, the time taken for the material present to double itself. Thus, Penfound & Earle (1948) reported the number of days taken for the numbers of plants of *Eichhornia crassipes* to double, though they did not give the method used to compute this. Gaudet (in press) working with *Salvinia minima* and *S. molesta* under standardized culture conditions also calculated doubling time in days for numbers of leaves using the formula :

$$\text{Doubling time} = \frac{\ln 2}{\dfrac{\ln N_1 - \ln N_o}{t_1 - t_o}} \tag{7}$$

By substitution from formula (3)

$$\text{Doubling time} = \frac{\ln 2}{RGR} \tag{8}$$

The concept of doubling time is also applied to the growth kinetics of micro-biological cultures of bacteria and algae where it is often referred to as generation time. Obviously, however, the concept is used for aquatic macrophytes without implication to the length of time between cell divisions.

Increments in dry weight are often measured to determine growth but, due to the utilization of part of the plant's carbohydrate in the process of respiration, such increments must be less than the original (gross) amount fixed. Such net production, however, is the basis for the growth of the plant. The International Biological Programme had as one of its objectives the standardization of methods of biological measurement and, in the handbook on primary production in aquatic environments (Vollenweider, 1969), Westlake (1969) recommends that the productivity of aquatic macrophytes be recorded in terms of unit weight per unit area of the earth's surface per unit time, i.e. g or kg/m^2 . day or t/ha . yr.

This is clearly appropriate for established stands of aquatic vegetation, as in a swamp, but such measurements are of less value in assessing the problem of mobile floating aquatic weeds when it is of greater interest to know the increase in plant numbers or area colonized. In this case, growth rate measurements may be more meaningful.

Penfound & Earle (1948) measured standing crops of *Eichhornia crassipes* at regular intervals during the growing season. Samples were separated into living and dead material and dried in an oven. In this way, they attempted to show the increasing percentage of living matter as well as the increase in the absolute value of this component during the growing season though it is probable that their calculations were based on too few samples. However, such measurements would indicate net productivity, though they would be subject to sampling errors, as well as to errors derived from loss due to grazing and breakage of plants.

Similar methods may be used with emergent macrophytes and suitable techniques are given by Milner & Hughes (1968) and in Vollenweider (1969). Providing there is no loss between sampling periods, net productivity would be equivalent to the change in biomass. It is desirable to minimize sampling error by taking a large number of samples. The number of samples required to provide a 95 per cent probability that the true value lies within 10 per cent of the recorded mean can be computed from the formula

$$n = t^2_{0.05} \cdot S^2 / E^2 \tag{9}$$

where n is the number of samples required to estimate the mean weight m of the population, with a 95 per cent chance that m lies between the limits of $\pm E$; E is the allowable error expressed as a fraction of the mean, e.g. ± 10 per cent, $E = 0.1$; S^2 is an estimate of the square of the standard deviation, i.e. the variance; $4 \approx (1.96)^2$ or t^2.

For the equation to hold accurately, t should be found from t-tables corresponding to the required confidence level and to $n - 1$ degrees of freedom. Since neither S^2 nor t^2 can be known exactly at the time when this calculation is needed, 4 is an adequate value to obtain useful answers; t^2 can be changed if a different level of confidence is required (Westlake, personal communication).

In many situations it is also possible to obtain an estimate of losses due to grazing, etc. In tropical and subtropical communities where there are relatively minor seasonal changes in biomass, such methods cannot be employed and rate of turnover must be measured instead (Westlake, 1969).

It is technically difficult to obtain reasonably accurate assessments of the species composition and size of submerged aquatic plant populations but various methods are discussed in Vollenweider (1969). Sampling methods operated from above the water have been developed (Forsberg, 1959) and underwater sampling by sub-aqua divers employing essentially terrestrial techniques has also been utilized (Nygaard, 1958). Aerial photographic methods have been used to assess submerged vegetation in streams (Edwards & Brown, 1960). Productivity measurements have also been made employing ^{14}C in special containers (Wetzel, 1964).

A useful technique for assessing the quantity of submerged vegetation in a shallow water body, where the plants can be seen from the surface, was developed by Way, Newman, Moore & Knaggs (1971). A number of evenly spaced transects are made across the water body and, at points equidistant from one another, the quantity of submerged vegetation is estimated on a six-point scale 0-5, varying from absence (0) to a very dense even growth (5). These estimates can then be plotted out on a plan or map of the sampling area as points of different sizes. Way *et al.* compiled a different chart for each species but, for some objectives, it would be possible to incorporate both quantity of plants and the composition of the population as pie-diagrams of different sizes at each sampling point.

Hoogers & van der Weij (1971) have described a method of assessing the changes in quantity and species composition of aquatic plants in shallow ditches by means of monthly 'time-tables'. The sampling site is visited once a month and the percentage cover estimated for each species on a twelve-point scale from absence to 100 per cent in intervals of varying groups of percentages (mostly 10 per cent in size). Times of flowering or sporulation are also recorded. Time-tables are then constructed for these observations, which show clearly the change in dominance of different species during the season, the response of the community to environmental changes (including weed-control treatments), and the seasonal behaviour of individual species.

Mitchell (1970) measured the colonization of Lake Kariba by *Salvinia molesta* by means of regular surveys from a fixed-wing aircraft flying about 300 m above the lake surface at an air speed of 200 to 250 km per hour. Three or four observers took part in the surveys, each independently mapping the areas of weed on to a scale map of the lake (Fig. 4). After each flight, the recordings were compared and a map compiled, which reflected the average results of all observers. The areas were then measured with a planimeter. There was probably an inherent error in these estimations of about 10 per cent, but the greater accuracy that could be obtained by an aerial photographic survey was not justified because a considerable variation in weed area can be caused in a short while by changes in wind strength and direction.

3.4.3   The growth of Salvinia spp. and Eichhornia crassipes

The application of some of the above methods and the results that may be obtained can be illustrated with reference to the notorious aquatic weeds, *Eichhornia crassipes* and *Salvinia* spp. *Salvinia molesta* was first seen on Lake Kariba in May 1959, five months after closure of the dam and, by 1962, was recorded to have covered an area of over 1,000 km^2 (Fig. 4). Between 9 April and 25 August 1960, the estimated area covered by *Salvinia* increased from 286 km^2 to 421 km^2. From 1963, the area of Lake Kariba suitable for colonization by *Salvinia* was limited mainly by wave action which increased as the lake reached full size (Mitchell, 1969).

The growth of individual plants was measured in the laboratory and in the lake itself (Mitchell & Tur, in preparation). The highest rates of growth were obtained in culture solution in the laboratory, where mean relative growth rates of up to 21.64 per cent per day in terms of leaf number and 17.16 per cent per day in terms of dry weight were achieved. Growth in field conditions was not as rapid and mean relative growth rates ranging between 8.61 per cent and 4.85 per cent per day, in terms of increase in leaf number, and 6.83 per cent and 4.04 per cent per day, in terms of dry weight, were achieved. Growth rates were higher when nutrients were more readily available and during the warmer times of the year.

The main difference between laboratory culture conditions and field growth conditions, which could have brought about a higher growth rate in the former, was the higher concentration of plant nutrients in the artificial culture solution. There is little doubt that nutrient availability is the factor most likely to limit the rate of growth of *Salvinia molesta*, when other conditions are suitable for the establishment of permanent mats of the plant.

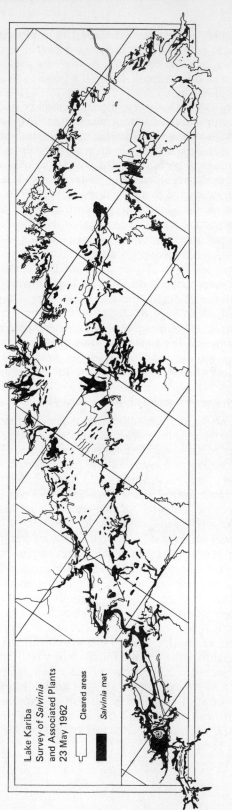

Lake Kariba
Survey of *Salvinia*
and Associated Plants
23 May 1962

☐ Cleared areas

■ *Salvinia* mat

Figure 4. A reduction from the original 1:250,000 *Salvinia* survey map for Lake Kariba recorded on 23 May 1962, one year before the lake reached full level. On this occasion the weed occupied 1,000 km² (21.5 per cent) of the lake surface.

Blackman (1960) obtained even higher values of 45 per cent per day for *Salvinia natans* in culture, but his experiments were carried out in richer nutrient solution and the most rapid growth was obtained at high temperatures and light values. These results also suggest that the availability of nutrients is an important requirement for the achievement of rapid rates of growth by this type of plant. Gaudet (in press) measured the growth of *S. minima* and *S. molesta* in sterile culture under simulated tropical conditions. The former species was recorded to have a doubling time of 4.0 days at the highest light intensity used. *S. molesta* produced leaves at a slower rate (doubling time = 4.6 days) but performed consistently better in terms of increase in dry weight and leaf area. Gaudet suggested that S. molesta is more successful as an aggressive weed than *S. minima* because the former produces larger leaf areas in the same light intensities during the same period of time.

The growth of *Eichhornia crassipes* has been measured by Bock (1969), who measured increase in wet weight and increase in plant numbers, at varying intervals from April to June and from April to October, during the growing season in California. The highest growth rates were obtained in May and June when daily increment factors for plant numbers were 1.066 and 1.077 ($\overline{RGR}$ = 6.4 per cent per day and 7.4 per cent per day) and for wet weight were 1.090 and 1.060 ($\overline{RGR}$ = 8.6 per cent per day and 5.8 per cent per day). Measurements in Jamaica gave a value of 1.104 ($\overline{RGR}$ = 9.9 per cent per day).

Evans (1963) recorded that 1,200 plants were produced by vegetative reproduction from two parent plants over a period of 130 days on the Congo River. Counts were made at periodic intervals and from these it can be calculated that $\overline{RGR}$ = 4.9 per cent per day for the whole period.

Penfound & Earle (1948) recorded the increase in number of plants from offshoots in *Eichhornia crassipes* between March and June in experimental pits. During this period, doubling time varied between 11 and 18 days, with an over-all average throughout the period of 12.5 days. Repetition of the experiment in subsequent years gave values for doubling time varying between 11.2 and 15.0 days. This can be compared with Parsons (1963) who reported a doubling period of about two weeks. Penfound & Earle also measured the rate of advance of a mat of *E. crassipes* over an open water surface and, during the growing season, showed this to have an average monthly value of 0.62 m (2.1 ft).

Westlake (1963) estimated that *Eichhornia crassipes* growing in good conditions in Louisiana (United States) would have a mean productivity during the growing season of 7.4 to 22 g/m^2 . day dry weight with an annual mean production of 15 to 44 t/ha . year dry weight.

3.5.   REGENERATION AND REPRODUCTION

One of the characteristics of a weed is its high reproductive capacity. Rates of vegetative reproduction of certain floating species were referred to in the previous section to exemplify methods of recording growth rate. In addition, the production of propagules and the ability of aquatic plants to regenerate from relatively small pieces needs to be considered, as well as reproduction from seeds or spores.

In many aquatic weeds, portions do not die when broken off from the parent plant but regenerate to form new plants. *Elodea canadensis, Lagarosiphon major* and *Egeria densa* have extended their influence in New Zealand because of the facility with which detached pieces form adventitious roots and become the foci of new infestations (Chapman, 1970). *Hydrilla verticillata,* a recent introduction to the

45

United States of America from the old world, behaves in the same fashion but, in addition, produces two types of specialized vegetative propagules. 'Tubers' are produced by subterranean shoots with swollen tips that are apparently able to lie dormant in the mud for some time during unfavourable conditions (Blackburn & Weldon, 1969a; Steward, personal communcation). Specialized dwarf shoots are also produced on normal stems. These are called turions and, when detached, can regenerate into new plants. As many as 1,000 turions or 'tubers' may be produced per square metre in one growing season (Blackburn & Weldon, 1969a). Several other species are capable of this mode of perennation and vegetative reproduction and Sculthorpe (1967) describes a number of examples of these.

As a consequence of the efficient production of large numbers of vegetative propagules many of the most dangerous aquatic weeds have become independent of sexual reproductive processes. The spread of *Elodea canadensis* through Western Europe and later in New Zealand apparently took place in the absence of male plants (Sculthorpe, 1967), and the same is true of *Lagarosiphon major* and *Egeria densa* in New Zealand (Mason, 1960 ; Chapman, 1970).

Loyal & Grewal (1966) and Mitchell (1970) showed that *Salvinia molesta* (cited as *S. auriculata*) is incapable of forming viable spores and Mitchell (in press, *b*), when describing this plant as *S. molesta*, advances the hypothesis that it is a sterile hybrid of possible horticultural origin. Herzog (1935) showed that portions of *S. auriculata* would regenerate, providing a bud was present. Mitchell (1970) carried out experiments on the regeneration of plants of *S. molesta* from various portions,each with an axillary of apical bud taken from plants of different ages, and showed that regeneration was 100 per cent successful in younger, larger portions. The percentage decreased when the plant portions were smaller or were taken from older parts of the plant. The production of vegetative propagules by aquatic plants is reviewed in some detail by Sculthorpe (1967), who shows that these are often produced in response to adverse environmental conditions and recommence growth when conditions improve. Many of these propagules can withstand desiccation which would kill normal vegetative growth. When these propagules are readily dispersed by water currents and other agents, such as birds and man, they are a potent means for promoting the dispersal of the species, especially when they are produced in large numbers.

Though there is a tendency among aquatic plants for the development of vegetative propagation, sometimes apparently accompanied by the dimunition in the importance of sexual reproduction, the importance of seed and spore formation must not be underestimated, especially as these are frequently adapted to withstand long periods of adverse conditions. Indeed, Datta & Biswas (1969) showed that the germination of seeds of *Pistia stratiotes* was enhanced by dry storage. Even a plant like *Eichhornia crassipes*, which has marked abilities for vegetative reproduction (section 3.4.2), is still capable of producing large numbers of seeds. Evans (1963) reported that a single ovary can produce as many as 500 ovules, though not all these are viable. Das (1968) showed that short periods of sub-freezing temperatures killed seeds as well as rhizomes and would clearly limit the plant's distribution in temperate regions. Hitchcock, Zimmermann, Kirkpatrick & Earle (1949) investigated the conditions for seedling germination and showed that moisture, high temperature and high light intensity were required. Pettet (1964) reported that conditions for seedling germination occur after spraying the plant with the herbicide 2,4–D on the River Nile because the dead plants are washed on to the river banks, thus concentrating the seeds. At the same time, the decaying plants provide an ideal condition for germination and growth of seedlings. *E. crassipes* seedlings have narrow strap-like leaves quite unlike those of the adult and therefore may not be recognized as such even when they do occur.

Yeo (1964) has shown that female spikes of *Typha latifolia,* which are 18 cm (7 in) in length, produce an average of over 222,000 seeds (range 117,000 to 268,000). Germination was generally poor unless the cells along the transverse edge of the seed were damaged by pressure, when 100 per cent success was achieved. One successfully germinated *Typha* seed gave rise to a plant which, within one growing season, produced a network of rhizomes covering an area 3.05 m (10 ft) in diameter with 98 aerial shoots of various sizes and 104 lateral buds. *Phragmites australis* generally exhibits poor seed germination and high seedling mortality in the field (Haslam, 1971*a*) but this seems to be of little disadvantage to the maintenance of stands of this plant, which have been estimated to be of the order of 1,000 years old in some cases (Rudescu, Niculescu & Chivu, 1965). Apparently spread is mainly by rhizome growth. Young rhizomes will grow rapidly in good nutrient and hydrological conditions and Haslam (1970*a*) has shown that a young clone established by a seed or rhizome can advance up to 2 m a year and produce up to about 200 shoots per m^2 in this advancing zone.

Many submerged and emergent aquatic plants show remarkable powers of regeneration after cutting (see Chapter 6). *Ranunculus* in the chalk streams of southern England will grow back to its former quantity within two months of cutting in the early part of the growing season (Westlake, 1968) and stands of *Phragmites* are harvested regularly once a year in the Danube delta without harming the plants (Rudescu *et al.,* 1965).

3.6 EFFECTS OF MAN-MADE DISTURBANCE

3.6.1 *Alteration of hydrological régime*

Aquatic weed growths, which occur after man-made disturbances of the natural hydrological régime, are often unexpected and frequently interfere with the proposed utilization of the water. For these reasons, such outbreaks attract a disproportionate amount of attention and comment. However, there is no doubt that by interfering with the established hydrological régime, man will often create conditions which will promote the rapid growth of aquatic plants that, previously, may have been rare, or no problem, in the locality.

Growths of plants in reservoirs and man-made lakes have been reported on a number of occasions (Little, 1966, 1969; Sculthorpe, 1967; van Donselaar, 1968; Mitchell, 1969, 1970, in press *a*; Holm, Weldon & Blackburn, 1969; Peltier & Welch, 1970; Chapman, 1970; Cook & Gut, 1971) and the growth of plants in irrigation canals is equally well known (Timmons, Bruns, Lee, Yeo, Hodgson, Weldon & Comes, 1963; Gupta, 1966; Bill, 1969; Holm *et al.,* 1969). Stabilization or diminution of water flow, control of water-level fluctuation and ensured continuity of water supply are all factors which potentially promote the growth of certain aquatic plants. These factors may also affect turbidity and water depth which would alter light quality in such a way as to promote the growth of a submerged plant, as occurs, for example, with *Elodea canadensis* in Great Britain (Haslam, 1971). Peltier & Welch (1969) and Haslam (1971) have investigated the factors that affect weed growth in rivers altered by interference or management by man. They show that the main effects are brought about by an alteration in physical factors, such as rate of flow, substrate texture and light penetration. Nutrient enrichment may also have an effect, as discussed in paragraph 3.6.3.

3.6.2 Plant invasions

Man's propensity for introducing plants and animals into areas where they are not native, and in which they are out of balance with the biological systems that have evolved there, has often caused serious problems, ultimately having an adverse effect on man's welfare. Elton's (1958) treatment of this topic and its ecological implications should be consulted for examples and detail. Aquatic plants provide some of the most spectacular examples of the adverse consequences of plant invasions as exemplified by the population explosions of *Salvinia molesta* and *Eichhornia crassipes* when taken out of the neotropics to tropical regions in other parts of the world. The spreads of *Azolla filiculoides* and *Elodea canadensis* in Europe and of *Elodea* and other Hydrocharitaceae in New Zealand are also illustrative of the phenomenon (Sculthorpe, 1967). Further examples are given by Ranwell (1967) and it is obvious that every attempt should be made to prevent the adventive spread of aquatic plants.

A study of the history of these introductions shows that four categories of people—aquarists, pisciculturists, botanists and horticulturists—are mainly responsible. Aquarists have established a world-wide trade in aquatic plants, in which noxious aquatic weeds are freely transferred from one country to another. Horticulturists and professional botanists have also been guilty of introducing potentially dangerous plants into countries where they do not naturally occur and in which they could flourish. For example *Eichhornia crassipes* is still advertised in some horticultural catalogues and *Salvinia molesta* was introduced to Sri Lanka by the University in Colombo for botanical studies (Williams, 1956).

Pisciculturists also assist in this process and *Elodea canadensis* was introduced into New Zealand from Tasmania in water containing perch, tench and goldfish (Thomson, 1922) and was planted in a pond with trout in 1868 (Armstrong, 1872). While one would not want to inhibit useful scientific research in any of these fields, scientists working with these plants should be made fully conversant with the risk and compelled to exercise the same degree of caution as they would with a dangerous pathogen. It is more difficult to justify these imports for purely commercial trade and authorities should give serious consideration to its abolition.

3.6.3 Nutrient enrichment

As stated in Chapter 1, addition of plant nutrients to a water body causes it to become eutrophic and increases its potential standing crop of plants. In standing waters, which tend to act as a sink for the nutrients draining into them from the surrounding catchment area, eutrophication is thought to be a process which occurs naturally over a long period of time, though there are indications that this may not always be so. Some authorities distinguish between the naturally occurring phenomenon and cultural eutrophication, the acceleration in this process which is brought about by the discharge of wastes from human society. However, if man is regarded as a component of the world ecosystem (as surely he must be) it is doubtful if this distinction has validity. Whatever view is taken of this, there is no doubt that eutrophication is promoted by man's activities and that it, in turn, promotes the growth of plants in aquatic ecosystems where they were previously absent, or only present in small numbers. Increasing public awareness of environmental degradation has brought this subject to the forefront and a number of symposia have been held recently to discuss the causes and consequences of eutrophication.

In tropical countries, plant nutrients are often the factors most likely to limit plant growth and thus the addition of nutrients to the system often produces spectacularly rapid results (e.g. Falconer, Marshall & Mitchell, 1970). Many tropical aquatic plants grow in waters where plant nutrients are constantly in demand and thus are adapted to respond rapidly to nutrients as they become available. For example, there is evidence that nitrogen is frequently the most likely limiting factor in tropical areas and *Salvinia molesta* responds to its availability by an increase in branching and other manifestations of rapid vegetative growth (Mitchell, 1970). However, it must not be thought that the effects of eutrophication are less pronounced in temperate regions. Chapman (1970) considered that the nutrient enrichment taking place in the Rotorua Lakes of North Island, New Zealand, had promoted the growth of aquatic weeds. Williams (1969) came to the same conclusion about the growth of aquatic macrophytes in the eutrophicated Lake Wendouree, Ballarat, Victoria, Australia. Most of the Central European lakes are also well known examples of eutrophicated lakes in the temperate zone.

3.7   LIMITING FACTORS TO AQUATIC WEED GROWTH

Preceding sections in this chapter have dealt with factors that promote the growth of aquatic plants and it is obvious that aquatic plants will be inhibited by trends in these factors in the opposite direction to that given in previous discussion. Thus low light values induced by turbidity and large phytoplankton growths, hydrological conditions that are adverse to a particular plant species or community and low nutrient values will all act as possible limiting factors to the growth and establishment of troublesome growths of aquatic weeds. However, in addition, there are some factors which have not yet been mentioned. Mitchell (1969, 1970, in press *b*) has shown that the quantity of *Salvinia molesta* on Lake Kariba was reduced by the physical effect of wave action and river floods which developed when the lake reached its full capacity. The presence of some form of anchorage which prevents floating plants from being moved by wind or water current is also important and the gradual breakdown of partially submerged trees on Lake Kariba is bringing about a reduction in the quantities of *Salvinia*.

The importance of physical and chemical factors in determining the quality of the environment and therefore the nature of aquatic plant growth cannot be too strongly stressed. But the role of other biotic components of the ecosystem as competitors and grazers must not be neglected. Many aquatic plant populations have arisen by vegetative reproduction from a single plant and such clones exhibit little genetic variability. Thus, they are particularly susceptible to disease or attacks from pathogenic organisms which, once established, encounter little resistance. Disease has been thought to be responsible for the decline in *Myriophyllum spicatum* in Chesapeake Bay on the east coast of the United States of America between 1963 and 1967 (Elser, 1969).

It may be possible to manipulate several of these factors so as to decrease or prevent problems caused by aquatic weeds and this subject is considered in Chapter 5.

4. The effects of excessive aquatic plant populations

D. S. Mitchell (United Kingdom)

4.1 INTRODUCTION

Large populations of aquatic plants may prevent or inhibit the utilization of water resources in a variety of ways, though the economic consequences of these effects are often difficult to evaluate. When money is available, there is sometimes a tendency to mount control measures without calculating the economic benefit which should result from the removal or limitation of the weeds in question. However, on the one hand, this calculation is often difficult because several types of water utilization are not easy to quantify in monetary terms and, on the other, prognoses of the consequences of not exercising available control measures can only be speculative.

Excessive populations of aquatic weeds may increase the loss of water from a water body by evapotranspiration; interfere with the movement of boats for recreation, transport and fishing; impede the flow of water in canals and rivers; interfere with the operation of hydro-electric and irrigation schemes; occupy useful volume in water storage facilities; prevent the operation of commercial fisheries; devalue waterfront properties; create stagnant conditions in water by the deposition of large amounts of organic matter and by the prevention of photosynthesis under dense floating mats; and, finally, shelter and promote the development of populations of disease vector animals. Guscio, Bartley & Beck (1965) reviewed some of the problems caused in the United States of America by obnoxious aquatic plants and Holm, Weldon & Blackburn (1969) discussed examples of difficulties caused by aquatic weeds in various parts of the world, while Little (1966, 1969) and Mitchell (in press *a*) have listed the problems caused by weeds in man-made lakes. There are relatively few objective estimates of the economic cost of an aquatic weed in a particular situation but Holm *et al.* (1969) cite an annual loss of $ 43 million from *Eichhornia crassipes* in the states of Florida, Alabama, Mississippi and Louisiana, in 1956. Some estimate of the cost of an aquatic weed problem may also be obtained from the cost of control measures on the assumption that this expenditure is justified by an economic benefit consequent on the control of the plant. On this basis, about U.S.$1 million (50 x 10^6 Belgian francs) were spent in the then Belgian Congo (now Zaire), in 1956 and 1957 in an unsuccessful attempt to control *Eichhornia crassipes* in the Congo River. One hundred and fifty tons of *E. crassipes* were still estimated to be passing through Stanleyville in the following year, though the river remained navigable (Lebrun, 1959). In the Sudan, weed control directed against *E. crassipes* in the Nile at one time reached $1.5 million a year (Holm *et al.,* 1969). The cost of keeping the weeds in check in a typical land drainage system in Britain in 1969/1970 was $388 per km (£240 per mile) in the main channels, $126 per km (£78 per mile) in the tributory drains and $65 per km (£40 per mile) in farm ditches; amounting to approximately $6.5 per ha (£1 per acre) of agricultural land in the most intensively drained areas (Robson, personal communication). In this chapter it is proposed to present some examples of the way in which aquatic weeds have adversely affected man's welfare and to discuss the consequences of these effects.

4.2 EVAPOTRANSPIRATION

It has been assumed by many workers that a dense stand of aquatic plants will lose more water to the atmosphere by transpiration than would normally be lost by evaporation from an open water surface occupying the same area. However, it is very difficult to make meaningful direct measurements of water loss by plants in natural situations as any interference with the plants will almost certainly affect their rate of transpiration. A number of formulae have been derived from which evaporation can be calculated indirectly from other related environmental weather factors such as temperature, humidity, etc. Penman (1963) reviewed the subject of vegetation and hydrology and discussed the application of such formulae. Recently, Linacre, Hicks, Sainty & Grauze (1970) compared evaporation from a *Typha* swamp with that from a nearby open lake, in an area of generally sparse rainfall in Australia, using an instrument called a Fluxatron, which correlates fluctuations in temperature and vertical wind to obtain the flux of sensible heat. Evaporation rates obtained from two other formulae, one based on bulk properties of the ambient air and the other on an energy/balance approach using the Bowen ratio, gave similar results.

Several workers have carried out direct measurements in a variety of natural and artificial conditions in which they have compared water lost from stands of aquatic plants with that lost from a comparable open water surface. While these may not be regarded as absolute values, it is possible that they indicate the factors which increase or decrease the difference between evapotranspiration from a stand of aquatic plants and evaporation from an open water surface.

Penfound & Earle (1948) compared water lost by tubs of water covered by *Eichhornia crassipes* with similar tubs of open water in an experiment carried out in the open in Louisiana (United States). Over a period of five weeks during November, the ratio of evapotranspiration to evaporation varied from 1.66 : 1 to 2.9 : 1, with a mean of 2.5 : 1. They repeated the experiment during summer (June/July) over a period of 33 days, during which rain fell on 21 days, and measured a mean ratio of evapotranspiration to evaporation of 3.2. : 1. During a period of ten days of reasonably clear weather towards the end of the experiment when the leaves on the plants had reached a length of about 50 cm, the ratio of evapotranspiration to evaporation was 6.6. : 1. Penfound & Earle's results indicated that the ratio of evapotranspiration to evaporation is increased by increase in temperature, by decrease in humidity and by increase in the vigour and size of the plants.

Little (1967) measured the evapotranspiration of *Eichhornia crassipes* and *Salvinia molesta* in greenhouse conditions in moving and still air. Using similar containers with open water surfaces as controls, he showed that the ratio of evapotranspiration to evaporation was 4-5 : 1 for *E. crassipes* and 1-2 : 1 for *S. molesta*. The ratios were increased by blowing air over the cultures with a fan. Mitchell (1970) carried out a series of measurements of evaporation and evapotranspiration in a randomized block experiment with dishes containing water only, water densely covered with *S. molesta* and water covered with *E. crassipes* bearing leaves about 20 cm long. Each treatment was replicated five times and the dishes re-randomized between each measurement.

The experiment was conducted in a greenhouse over a period of forty days in early summer and the ratio of evapotranspiration of *Salvinia* to evaporation from the open water surface ranged from 0.45 : 1.00 to 1.80 : 1.00, with a mean of 1.14 : 1.00. Similar values for *E. crassipes* were 1.45 : 1.00 to 1.98 : 1.00 with a mean of 1.62 : 1.00. Humidities were generally high and guttation was occasionally observed to take place from some of the *E. crassipes* plants.

Timmer & Weldon (1967) carried out measurements, also with *E. crassipes,* of the ratio of evapotranspiration to evaporation during March in Florida. Plants were grown in four fertilized growth pools until the leaves had reached a length of 75 cm. The losses of water from these containers were compared with losses of water from two similar growth pools containing water only. The loss of water from the latter was found to be comparable to values obtained for free water evaporation from Class A aluminium pans. Timmer & Weldon obtained a ratio of 3.7 parts water lost by evapotranspiration to one part lost by a free water surface. Treatment of the *E. crassipes* with the herbicide, 2,4–D, reduced water losses from the dishes containing the plants.

Evapotranspiration losses from emergent species and phreatophytes growing on the margins of the water body are more difficult to measure directly. Guscio *et al.* (1965) reported that phreatophytes (excluding beneficial species) cover about 6.5×10^6 ha (16×10^6 acres) in the seventeen western states of the United States of America and annually lose 30.65 km^3 (25×10^6 acre ft). They also reported that *Typha* spp. use 211 to 254 cm (83 to 100 in) of water every year. This compares with evaporation rates of 127 to 190 cm (50 to 75 in) from open water surfaces. Rudescu, Niculescu & Chivu (1965) reported that the annual evapotranspiration from a dense *Phragmites* stand is 1.0 to 1.5 m and Haslam (1970*b*) has noted that dense stands of this species in East Anglia (England), lose more water through evapotranspiration than is supplied by rain. She reports that *Phragmites* have been used to aid the draining of ponds in the Netherlands.

Burian (1971) has carried out a large number of *in situ* measurements of transpiration in a reed swamp fringing the lake Neusiedler See, Austria, and these are likely to be more indicative of actual loss than the experimental measurement sited earlier. He found that, on the average, 1 m^2 of reed consumed 1 m^3 of water in 190 days during the period of main growth. Less than half of this loss was supplied by rain. At the same time, evaporation from the free surface of the lake and the free water surface in the reed swamp was 700 mm and 400 mm respectively. Burian also illustrated a nomogram in which transpiration is plotted against the temperature and the relative humidity of the air so that if the latter two values are determined the first can be calculated.

Against these results, Linacre *et al.* (1970) found that evapotranspiration from the swamp they worked with (E_S) was less than that from the lake (E_W) during dry periods ($E_S : E_W =$ about 1 : 1.6 and 1 : 3), but was more or less the same following rainfall which saturated the surrounding countryside. This confirms results obtained by Rijks (1969) from an African papyrus swamp using a heat budget approach where $E_S : E_W$ ratios averaged about 0.6. Linacre *et al.* considered that the lower rate of evaporation in the swamp appeared to be due to a combination of sheltering of the water surface by the reeds, their higher degree of reflectivity (albedo) and their internal resistance to water movement during dry periods. They concluded that 'in dry climates at least, it is likely that growth of reeds in a lake or other water body will reduce rather than increase the water loss'.

Evapotranspiration losses from aquatic weeds are clearly important, particularly in arid regions where water is limiting development and evaporation rates are high.

Contrary to expectations, it appears that, in this situation, reed-swamp vegetation may drecrease over-all water loss and it would be interesting to know whether floating vegetation would behave the same way.

4.3 IMPEDIMENT TO FLOW AND OCCUPATION OF USEFUL VOLUME

Submerged aquatic weeds do not increase water losses from a water body but may trap silt, may impede flow in a canal or river and may occupy useful volumes of water in small water-storage reservoirs. Water flow is affected when plants reduce the cross-section of a canal or river and Guscio *et al.* (1965) reported studies which showed that plant growths in varying density and size may reduce the design flow rate for an artificial canal by as much as 97 per cent. Timmons (1960) stated that, of the approximately 232,000 km (144,000 miles) of canals and ditches in the seventeen western states of the United States of America, about 76,000 km (47,000 miles) were infested with growths of submerged aquatic plants. Eight million dollars a year were spent controlling these and in some cases this was as much as 40 per cent of the annual operation and maintenance costs of irrigation schemes. Emergent species also cause similar difficulties and, in addition, act as a trap for silt, causing sedimentation which is impossible to deal with while the plants remain. Floating species restrict flow to a lesser extent but, when massed in a thick mat, create friction losses similar to those provided by the sides and bottom of the canal. For example, Guscio *et al.* (1965) cited a study which showed that a dense mat of *Eichhornia crassipes* covering canals in the Everglades in Florida, reduced the efficiency of large canals to 40 per cent, while small canals were reduced by up to 80 per cent of flow capacity.

Little (1966) noted that large volumes of water contained in a lake could be occupied and displaced by aquatic vegetation and estimated that, in Lake Rio Lempa, in El Salvador, 405 ha (1,000 acres) of *Eichhornia crassipes* displaced 1,226 m³ (1,000 acre feet) of water. Westlake (1965) cites estimates of volumes for several submerged species ranging from 0.6 (*Chara*) to 1.6 (*Potamogeton pectinatus*) 1/kg wet weight. Westlake (1968) calculated that standing crops of submerged aquatic plants in the River Frome were 13 to 24 t/ha. The total area of the main channels in the river was estimated at approximately 43 ha, so that if the higher figure is taken the total weight of weed present would be 112 t, which would occupy a volume of 118 m³. The discharge of the River Frome is 2.8 to 17 m³/sec and thus, even at lowest flow levels, the volume of water equivalent to that occupied by the weed present will be discharged in 42 seconds. In summer, when the flow is least, the weed is estimated to occupy about 0.3 per cent of the river volume. Therefore, it would appear that aquatic weeds would not be a particular nuisance, in respect of occupation of useful volume, except in very small water bodies where storage of water was critical.

4.4 INTERFERENCE WITH BOAT MOVEMENT AND ASSOCIATED UTILIZATION OF WATER RESOURCES

Established stands of aquatic macrophytes of all life forms can prevent the passage of conventional boats. Submerged weeds will foul the propellers of conventional, motor-driven craft, if they rise close enough to the surface. For this reason, mechanical paddles and other special methods of propulsion for waterweed-cutting boats have been developed (see Chapter 6) and, in the Everglades of Florida (United States) aircraft engines driving air propellers have been mounted on flat-bottomed boats, which can then move in very shallow water full of aquatic plant growth.

Some of the most serious problems are caused by floating masses of vegetation. Because of their mobility, these can be blown into a harbour or channel and completely fill it in a matter of hours. Initially, a temporary mat, such as this, will not impede the passage of large powerful boats, but it is a considerable nuisance and, if allowed to stabilize, may become impenetrable. Harbours and narrow channels have been affected in this way by extensive floating mats of *Salvinia molesta* on Lake Kariba, and Devil's Gorge at the top of the lake has been periodically blocked by a compacted mat of plants blown into the gorge. At these times, the hydrofoil passenger service has to be suspended temporarily above the Devil's Gorge.

Floating weeds also cause serious problems in rivers. *Eichhornia crassipes* had already begun to block transporation in the Congo River in 1954, only two years after it was first reported (Holm *et al.*, 1967). Gay (1960) reported that, on the Nile, river steamers were being delayed by approximately one day on an eleven-day run by November 1958, less than two years after the probable introduction of the plant into the system.

Boats are used for a multitude of purposes and therefore weed interference with boat movement is often serious from several points of view. Commercial fisheries can not obtain access to fishing areas and, in addition, are unable to operate their gear. Recreational use is seriously inhibited, if not completely prevented. The increasing importance of water for recreation is becoming apparent, especially in countries where open water surfaces are limited and where standards of living are high. Holm *et al.* (1969) figure the example of a $900,000 resort motel which was built on the banks of a river and which was forced into bankruptcy eighteen months after opening because an invasion of *Hydrilla* prevented the use of the waterway. Lake McIlwaine, an impoundment near Salisbury, Rhodesia, with a heavy recreational use was recently threatened by floating mats of *Eichhornia crassipes* and, on this occasion, it was estimated that investment in recreational use of the lake amounted to about U.S.$3 million, which would have been adversely affected had the *Eichhornia crassipes* been allowed to increase unchecked.

4.5 HEALTH

Aquatic plants provide both habitat and food for the animal vectors of human diseases such as malaria, filaria, fascioliasis and schistosomiasis (bilharziasis). The first two are carried by mosquitoes, the larvae of which breed in the calm, still pockets of water created among stands of floating vegetation and emergent vegetation. Malarial parasites are carried by *Anopheles* mosquitoes and Rozeboom & Hess (1944) have shown that the breeding of *A. quadrimaculatus* in the Tennessee Valley (United States) is related to the extent that plant organs intersect the water surface. They found strong correlation between a high value for this intersection line per unit area and a high population density of anopheline larvae. Studies on the phenology of plants in the Tennessee Valley Authority reservoirs in Alabama by Penfound, Hall & Hess (1945) showed that the development of some of these (e.g. *Saururus cernuus*) could be adversely affected by controlled water-level fluctuations during the growing season, while others such as *Typha latifolia* required a combination of water-level manipulation with pulling, cutting and grazing of the plants. Malaria had been prevalent in the Tennessee Valley but, assisted with this type of information, the Tennessee Valley Authority has been able virtually to eliminate the disease from the area by a programme of improved sanitation and reservoir management, involving a combination of shoreline management, treatment of certain areas with larvacide chemicals and carefully timed adjustments of the water level.

Mosquitoes are also responsible for transmitting various types of filariasis, the main vectors being species of *Anopheles, Culex* and *Mansonia.* Rural filariasis in Sri Lanka is caused by a human parasite, for which the intermediate host is the *Mansonia* mosquito. Williams (1956) notes that, though *Pistia stratiotes* is the main aquatic plant on which the mosquitoes breed, it was feared that *Salvinia,* which was present on the island in large quantities (it was estimated to have affected 8,910 ha (22,000 acres) of cultivable paddy fields and at least 810 ha (2,000 acres) of water-ways) would contribute to the build-up of a heavy perennial population of adult mosquitoes. In the United States, *Mansonia* is responsible for the transmission of encephalitis. These insects are associated with several vascular hydrophytes, the larvae being equipped with specialized breathing tubes which penetrate the plant tissue and obtain their air supplies from the air canals within the plant. These insects are not open to control by larvicides because of this behaviour and the only feasible means of limiting them is to destroy their plant habitat (Guscio *et al.,* 1965).

Fascioliasis, a disease caused by an infection of liver fluke, *Fasciola spp.,* is also associated with aquatic vegetation. In this case the disease, which may infect both man and cattle, is transmitted by a snail vector, *Limnaea spp.* The infection is acquired when plants, such as watercress (*Nasturtium officinale*) are eaten. In parts of Europe, this is especially common when plants are derived from beds fertilized with cattle dung. In Asia a similar intestinal fascioliasis is acquired by people eating water-chestnut (*Trapa spp.*).

Schistosomiasis is one of the most critical health problems of the tropics at this present time and the World Health Organization estimated that at least 150 million people were infected with the disease in 1965 (Jordan & Webbe, 1969). However, until recently, the disease has not received the same intensity of attention as some other tropical diseases, because of its insidious nature. Nevertheless, its debilitating effect on the general health of those infected with it and its widespread incidence (as much as 95 per cent in some populations) has undoubtedly serious consequences. Schistosomiasis induces general lethargy and shortens life expectancy and has there-fore inhibited improvements in the welfare of affected populations. The inter-mediate hosts in this case are species of the aquatic snails *Bulinus, Biomphalaria* and *Oncomelania.* These snails live in the microhabitats provided by aquatic vegetation in which they find both shelter and food in the form of epiphytic algae and detritus. Their eggs are laid on the surface of the plants and the life cycle of the animal thus depends to a considerable extent on the presence of suitable aquatic vegetation. However, the relationship between the snails and the vegetation is complex and it is difficult to define clear causal links (Jordan & Webbe, 1969). The possibility of contracting schistosomiasis from Lake Kariba was substantially increased after the lake level stabilized with the consequent development of extensive populations of submerged aquatic plants and therefore of snails. The floating mats of *Salvinia* do not appear to be particularly favoured by the snails, though they may be rapidly dispersed by mobile plants. This increasing risk necessitated the use of a molluscicide (Bayluscide) in those areas subject to considerable recreational use. The reported effect of this chemical on the *Salvinia* caused Wild & Mitchell (1970) to carry out investigation which showed that the chemical is more toxic to *Salvinia molesta* than to most other aquatic vegetation and this weed can be killed by concentrations of the order of 2.0 ppm.

The incidence of schistosomiasis is likely to increase wherever human populations, particularly with low standards of hygiene and sewage disposal, come into regular contact with permanent water, in which stands of aquatic vegetation support large populations of the required genera of snails. Water conservation by means of man-made lakes and the development of irrigation schemes in tropical areas with its attendant construction of permanent waterways have undoubtedly assisted the spread of the disease, as is shown by its increasing incidence in Brazil and parts of Africa.

Dawood, Farooq, Dazo, Miquel & Unrau (1965) have shown that in Egypt the bilharzial snails prefer *Potamogeton crispus,* followed by *E. crassipes* and then *Panicum repens*. Whereas the other plants are attached, *E. crassipes* is free floating and will therefore assist in spreading the disease and reinfecting areas which may have been subjected to recent control measures.

4.6   WATER RESOURCES MANAGEMENT

In addition to the specific effects and disadvantages of large populations of aquatic plants described in the preceeding pages, vascular hydrophytes may interfere with programmes of water-resource utilization and management. Chapman (1970) describes the problems caused in the operation of the Waikato hydro-electric system in New Zealand by drifting masses of *Ceratophyllum* and, occasionally, *Lagarosiphon* fouling the power-water intakes. Fears have been expressed that the functioning of the hydro-electric power stations on Lakes Kariba and Brokopondo (Surinam) would be adversely affected by *Salvinia molesta* and *Eichhornia crassipes* respectively. In neither case has this materialized, because of the depth of the intakes in the former and the control of the weed by herbicide in the latter. Aquatic plants also interfere with the operation of pumps in irrigation schemes by clogging filters and water intakes, thus increasing maintenance expenses.

Large stands of aquatic plants act as a reservoir of plant nutrient chemicals and so have the potential to stabilize nutrient-enriched waters in opposition to attempts to decrease the productivity of systems where this is undesirably high. Aquatic ecosystems are often associated with desirable wild-life habitats and the management of these may be made more difficult than it already is by the presence of excessive populations of aquatic plants. However, it is important to realize that an intricate and complex relationship exists between the various biological components of the system and it is essential to know something of these relationships before mounting extensive control campaigns against the offending vegetation.

5. Environmental management in relation to aquatic weed problems

D. S. Mitchell (United Kingdom)

5.1 INTRODUCTION

The main, and perhaps the most obvious, ways in which problems caused by excessive aquatic plant populations can be dealt with, are the institution of various chemical, mechanical or biological control measures. These will be described and discussed in Chapter 6. However, it may be possible, and often more desirable, to effect control by indirect methods, involving the manipulation of certain environmental factors. Such an approach demands a knowledge of the relationship between the species of plant or the plant community, which is causing the problem, and the environmental factors, which it is possible to manipulate. Furthermore, it is necessary to understand how different levels of the manipulated factors will affect other components of the ecosystem. Also it is important to consider the holocoenotic nature of the ecosystem (Fig. 2) when designing environmental management procedures. Finally, it is essential to monitor changes that are taking place, not only in the vegetation, but also in other critical and/or especially sensitive components of the system, so that the manipulative procedures may be properly regulated.

Manipulation of the environment to achieve certain objectives is one of the characteristics of modern man and, for example, forms the basis of much of agricultural practice. However, most of man's experience in this field has been gained with simplified ecosystems and the art of successful management of complex natural and semi-natural systems with large numbers of species still has to be achieved. There is no doubt that progress in this field, as in many others, is taking place largely by trial and error. Unfortunately, because of rapidly increasing pressure on environmental resources by the exponentially increasing human population, there is now no room for manoeuvre and errors cannot be afforded. This situation demands that a high priority be given to research aimed at understanding the complexities and interrelationships of our environment. However, progress and betterment of the human race cannot wait for the results of these investigations. Procedures of environmental management have to be designed and instituted on the basis of present knowledge, however inadequate, and this situation makes it essential for continuous environmental monitoring to form part of the management programme. As a corollary, any management procedures, worked out on the basis of information acknowledged to be inadequate, must be flexible and include viable alternatives, so that these can be readily introduced if unforeseen developments occur. Civil engineers and hydrologists, when planning man-made lakes or systems of irrigation canals, must be complemented by ecologists and hydrobiologists who supply expertise on the ecological impact of the former's designs and advise on their modification, if this is thought necessary. Furthermore, the management staff of the completed project should include appropriate ecologists who would monitor changes and co-operate in adjusting management procedures so that these have the least deleterious effect on the environment while remaining compatible with the stated objectives of the project.

White (1969) examined the strategies that have been employed in water resource management in the United States of America and pointed out the need for concern with water quality and sound management. He considered that 'it is more likely that human welfare in the United States will be impaired through degradation of water quality or through inept management than from a physical scarcity of water'. Strategies were defined as distinctive combinations of aims, means and decision criteria and White distinguished six main types in the United States. The history and development of these were reviewed and discussed in a way that has broad implications to water management policies in countries other than the United States. However, little attention was paid to the effects and consequences of aquatic vegetation on water resources.

The effects of various environmental factors on the growth of aquatic plants are discussed by Gessner (1955, 1959) and Sculthorpe (1967) and were briefly considered in Chapter 1. Those factors which promote excessive plant populations were discussed in more detail in Chapter 3. Some of these factors could be manipulated in such a way as to minimize water-weed problems and possible techniques and practices for the 'environmental engineer' to utilize in relation to aquatic macrophytes will be reviewed and discussed in this chapter. Consideration will be given to the management of existing water bodies, procedures for projected water bodies and the procedures to be adopted once an aquatic weed problem has been identified. At the outset however, it is essential to emphasize the absolute necessity of clearly defining the aims and objectives of the management policy before procedures to carry it into effect are worked out.

5.2   THE MANAGEMENT OF EXISTING WATER BODIES

Each stream, river, pond or lake, is composed of its own particular set of environmental and biotic components which give it a uniqueness similar to that of an individual in a population of the same species. Thus, while general principles can be deduced for the management of water resources for specific objectives, these may require modification in the light of local circumstances.

5.2.1   *Water pollution*

Water has long been regarded as an agent for waste disposal by human society and is likely to remain so for some time. The resultant pollution is a world-wide problem that commands the attention of all those responsible for the management of water resources. Hynes (1960) described the history and effect of different types of water pollution mainly with reference to English conditions and showed that the deposition of waste matter and other substances, such as pesticides, in water leads to detrimental changes in the aquatic ecosystem. Water pollution is difficult to define but, generally, can be taken to be the alteration of the water resource in some way as to make it less favourable to man. However, as in the decision of whether a certain plant is a weed, the application of such a definition depends upon a clear evaluation of the potential and actual uses of the water body in question, as well as a knowledge of the long- and short-term ecological effects of the possible polluting substance on the whole system.

Assessment of the biological effect of water pollution is also complicated by the natural evolution of water bodies. Both rivers and lakes change on a geological time scale. A river by its action alters the topography of the land and thus its flow patterns, while a lake is a transitory feature in a geological sense and is gradually filling in. Many of man's so-called pollution effects merely serve to accelerate the latter process and Hynes (1960) argues that a mere change in rate of a process which is occurring naturally should not be regarded as pollution. However, many of these changes result in a water body that is less favourable to man and, in this sense, they must be considered as pollution, especially when the rate has been grossly accelerated. Thus, on the one hand, rapid siltation as the result of poor land-use practices in the catchment and, on the other, rapid enrichment, leading to undesirable eutrophic conditions in a lake as a result of the discharge of nutrient-rich effluents, must both count as forms of water pollution.

Water can be polluted by the addition of a large number of substances, which, for convenience, can be grouped into eight categories.

1. Effluents containing inert suspended matter may be derived from sand washing and other washing processes in mining and quarrying. When produced in large quantities the suspended substances will smother submerged plants, though, generally, the particles eventually settle out at a rate depending on the degree of water turbulence.

2. Oil is capable of spreading over large areas of the air/water interface, even if added in very small amounts. By interfering with gaseous exchange at this interface, oil has adverse effects on submerged plants, though it has most serious effects on floating vegetation, which it usually kills.

3. Toxic substances occur in the waste waters produced by many industrial processes and include cyanides, arsenical compounds, heavy metals, acids, alkalis and poisonous organic substances such as phenols. Seidel (1971) has shown that certain species of emergent aquatic plants demonstrate surprising tolerance to some of these substances and may provide a means of handling such effluents (see Chapter 7).

4. Pesticides may be added directly to the water body in an attempt to control particular plant or animal pests, or may enter accidentally by run-off from agricultural land, overflow from cattle dips, or wind drift from aerial application to crops. Clearly, herbicides will kill sensitive plants if the chemical is present in lethal concentrations and will have adverse effects at lower quantities. Plants that are not sensitive to the particular chemical will be affected indirectly, through the changes in the biotic components of the system induced by the pesticide (Muirhead-Thomson, 1971).

5. Inorganic reducing substances, such as sulphites, absorb oxygen owing to a chemical oxygen demand. Such substances are present in the effluents of certain industrial processes. Excessive deoxygenation will kill aquatic plants, if exposure is prolonged, but it is often accompanied by other chemical changes, such as in pH and it is difficult to separate these effects.

6. *Organic substances* undergo bacterial decomposition and thus create a biological oxygen demand (BOD), which can be measured and used as a test of effluent quality. Effluents from several industrial processes, such as those used in sugar mills, breweries and paper mills, are rich in organic matter but perhaps the most important discharge in this category is sewage. Mineralization of these substances will result in increases in nutrient ions and consequently in plant populations. However this usually takes place some distance below the discharge point after the main deoxygenation effects have ameliorated.

7. *Effluent rich in plant nutrients,* such as purified sewage effluent, which has been treated to the secondary stage in a conventional sewage treatment plant, may bring about marked increases in aquatic plant populations.

8. *Hot-water effluents* are produced by atomic and other power plants and by certain industrial processes. Depending on the source, such effluents may contain dead organic matter from plants and animals killed in the heating process, as well as toxic chemicals. By changing the temperature régime of the water in the vicinity of their discharge point, these effluents may cause certain plants to be eliminated and allow others to become established. For example, in the United Kingdom, certain tropical plants now occur in such situations (Hynes, 1959).

It is not possible nor appropriate to consider all the biological effects of these pollutants in detail and readers are referred to Hynes (1959, 1960) for comprehensive accounts of these. Suffice to say that, in most cases, there is progressive dilution of the substances and their effects in running-water systems. Lakes differ in that the pollution substances accumulate in the system. However, many of the chemical substances break down and become innocuous, or sediment out on the lake bottom. An important exception is the addition of nutrient chemicals which are taken up in the biotic components of the system and lead to greatly increased standing crops, which may assume nuisance proportions. Thus, while pollution control must be an essential part of any management policy for a water body, it is especially important that nutrient inflows be continually monitored, if nuisance weed growths are to be prevented (see section 5.2.1.3).

5.2.2 Catchment effects

In addition to the more obvious effects of pollution, water is affected in a multitude of ways by human activity in the catchments. Cultivation may lead to increased soil erosion and therefore silt load ; agriculture involving the use of fertilizers often increases the nutrient content of water entering the system from such land (Biggar & Corey, 1969); forestation decreases and deforestation increases average flow and spates, as well as affecting the concentrations of dissolved chemicals (Cooper, 1969); grazing pressure on grassland and burning of vegetation, either accidental, or in connexion with certain agricultural practices, also affects run-off and concentrations of dissolved substances. Run-off is also affected by soil type, topography and type of precipitation, so that quantitative comparisons of the effects of different management régimes on catchments, even in the same locality, are very difficult. Betson, Eklund, Joyce, Kilmer, Lutz, Mason, McCraken, Nelson & Woodhouse (1970) discussed the problems of investigating these factors in a final report presenting the results of twenty years research in western North Carolina (United States). Among their findings was the important confirmation of 'the critical role which man occupies in the relationship between the land and the water'. As they pointed out, this implies that management of the water resource ultimately depends on the wise use of land in the catchment. A full consideration of this lies outside the scope of this manual but the importance of sound land management based on scientific knowledge must be emphasized.

5.2.3. *Nutrient supplies*

The effect of increased supplies of plant nutrients to the system has already been stated. In crude general terms, plants require water, light and nutrients for good growth and, in many aquatic situations, the first two are present by virtue of the existence of the water body and, therefore, are not normally open to manipulative control. However, this is less true of nutrients, the quantity of which can be affected by man's activities.

The trophic status of a lake depends on the availability of plant nutrients in the system. These can be supplied from sources within the system, such as decaying animal and vegetable matter (Jewell, 1970), or bottom muds (Mortimer, 1941, 1942). The processes involved in these cycles are complex and incompletely understood, even for systems where they have been studied in some detail. In any case, there usually appears to be a continuous loss of important nutrients through outflows, or by sedimentation into bottom muds or through being taken up into refractory organic matter (Jewell, 1970; Mitchell, 1970). Therefore sources outside the system are necessary to maintain the trophic status. These include allochthonous material, such as dead leaves and other organic matter washed into the system. This decays in the water, releasing nutrients as it does so, and this source is frequently important in small or running water systems. However, the most important external source is usually the nutrient content of the water flowing into the system. For example, Edmondson (1970) showed that, in Lake Washington, the standing crop of algae was strongly correlated to the phosphate concentration of the water which, in turn, was affected by concentration in the inflows. Thus, as the quantity of sewage and therefore phosphate entering the lake was decreased, the concentration of phosphate in the water became less and the algal standing crop declined.

Different systems are likely to react in different ways to these sources of supply. For example, shallow lakes, where turbulence can penetrate to the bottom deposits, will differ from deep lakes, where this does not occur over the major part of the lake, and these, in turn, will differ from man-made lakes, which generally have short retention times. Also, deep lakes will differ according to their mixing characteristics and the degree to which bottom waters become deoxygenated. Nevertheless, in spite of these differences, it is clear that in all these cases large standing crops of plants (whether algae or macrophytes) are likely to occur when nutrients are readily available. Thus, where excessive populations of weeds occur and where it is desirable to minimize stands of such plants, management procedures must include controls of the quantity of plant nutrients supplied to the system. Legislation attempting to regulate permissible concentrations of nutrients discharged into water must bear in mind that, in some cases and especially where standing bodies of water are concerned, cumulative totals may be more important than concentration in the effluents.

Considerable discussion has been held to ascertain which nutrients are generally more important for plant growth in aquatic systems. If this were known, control could be simplified by concentrating attention on the nutrient most likely to limit plant growth and, therefore, most likely to stimulate it when supplied in larger quantities than normal. Four elements, nitrogen, phosphorus, carbon and sulphur were mentioned in Chapter 1 and, in most cases, it will probably be necessary to ascertain which nutrient is the most important for a particular system through experimentation, either by fertilization experiments with lake water (see Lund, 1969) or by use of standard bioassay techniques (Malony, Miller & Blind, 1972).

In addition to nutrient control of inflows, careful attention should be paid to shoreline areas to minimize risk of excessive addition of allochthonous nutrient-rich matter to the system. Other ameliorative measures could include harvesting and removal of standing crops of plants and animals from the water and the manipulation of outflows from the system, so as to draw on layers which contain the most nutrients. Removal of plants and animals from the system may have economic benefits if these can be utilized (see Chapter 7).

5.2.4 *Water-level fluctuations*

Water depth and the extent to which water level fluctuates are factors that have considerable effects on the growth of a wide variety of aquatic plants. Furthermore, these factors are more open to manipulative control than many others. Sculthorpe (1967) described the effect of changes in water depth on aquatic plants of different life forms with reference to a number of examples. Penfound, Hall & Hess (1945) examined the effect of changes in lake level on the shoreline vegetation in the Tennessee Valley Authority reservoirs in Alabama. They differentiated three phases of fluctuation: recession, when the water level is dropping; progression, when it is rising; and cyclical fluctuation, when there is a regular rise and fall of about 0.3 m per week. Gradual recession of about 1 m in extent resulted in a lakeward extension of all three types of plants they distinguished; namely aquatic, wetland and terrestrial. Rapid, extensive recessions destroyed submerged and many floating and emergent aquatic species but promoted the germination and establishment of many wetland and terrestrial species in the zone of fluctuation. Progression of water level caused a shift of plant types in a shoreward direction. Terrestrial and some wetland species were destroyed. The germination of the seeds and the growth of perennating organs of most of these species were also prevented. Cyclical fluctuations allowed wetland species to become established to a level about 15 cm below the upper level of the cycle, while submerged aquatic species were able to establish themselves to a somewhat lower level. Thus, it is apparent that rapid and extensive fluctuations are more likely to have destructive effects on the shoreline vegetation than gradual changes of limited amount. However, a large number of vascular hydrophytes are able to adapt to the absence of free water by the production of land forms. Sculthorpe (1967) described the nature of these changes and gave a number of examples. This ability which is often associated with changes in the appearance of the plant must be borne in mind when assessing the effect of water-level fluctuations on aquatic weeds. For example, *Myriophyllum spicatum,* which is normally a submerged plant, is able to produce a reduced land form that enables the plant to withstand long periods without free water. Similarly, *Ludwigia stolonifera,* which is normally emergent, is able to produce both a free-floating form and a reduced land form. Free-floating forms, such as *Salvinia molesta, Eichhornia crassipes* and *Pistia stratiotes* are also capable of existing on moist soil in a reduced form particularly in humid conditions. For example, during the last ten years at least, *Salvinia molesta* has been growing on the edge of the rain forest opposite the Victoria Falls, above Lake Kariba, where it is kept continuously moist by the spray from the Falls.

The seasonal fluctuations in water level that occur in lakes are unlikely to be rapid or extensive enough to adversely affect marginal vegetation. However, man-made lakes are often characterized by a marked draw-down and thus a shoreline that is barren of plant growth. Furthermore, the means of manipulating water levels is usually present in a man-made lake. Seasonal fluctuations in rivers may also be gradual but, in areas where there is a marked seasonal distribution of rainfall, as in the savannah areas of Africa, the rivers are seasonal flash-flood rivers, which consequently support very little emergent and submerged vegetation. Man-made canals, on the other hand, are unlikely to be capable of fluctuations in water level that would be extensive enough to inhibit aquatic plant growth.

The different life forms of aquatic macrophytes, distinguished in Chapter 1, differ from one another, mainly in respect of their relationship to water depth. Thus, as shown above, fluctuations in water level have different effects on the different life forms and it will be convenient to consider these separately in relation to possible control.

1. Phreatophytes. These are difficult to control by manipulation of environmental factors. Many are able to withstand considerable periods with minimum water supplies and some can withstand submergence to a surprising extent. Riparian trees such as *Acacia albida* which were submerged by the rising waters of Lake Kariba were still alive three and four months after they had been 50 per cent or more under water. However, continuous submergence will apparently kill these plants if sufficiently prolonged. Thus, if elimination of phreatophytes is desired, retention of a high water level for a long period may be useful, though this is not likely to be possible in many natural or artificial water bodies.

2. Emergent aquatic plants. These are more dependent on water level than phreatophytes and, for example, have not yet become well established in Lake Kariba, ten years after the lake reached full level, because of the annual fluctuations of three or more metres in water level. *Typha* has been controlled by manipulating water levels (Steenis, Lawrence & Cofer, 1959) and it would seem likely that many emergent species could be controlled by rapid extensive changes in water level. These fluctuations need only take place at infrequent intervals, though vegetation would gradually become established on the zone of fluctuation during the intervening period.

3. Attached plants with floating leaves. These are also sensitive to excessive fluctuations in water level though they are able to adapt to a gradual rise in level by the unusual ability of mature petioles to lengthen by both cell elongation and cell division (Sculthorpe, 1967). Exposure to the air by a recession in water level will cause fairly rapid desiccation of leaves and flowering parts but the underground rhizomes are likely to be more resistant, depending on the degree of their submergence in the substrate and the ambient climatic conditions. However, Sculthorpe (1967) pointed out that floating leaved plants are restricted to rather narrow ecological limits where water of 0.5 m to 3.5 m deep is stationary or very slow-moving over stable silted substrates. However, where they have established populations of nuisance proportions, changes in water level are unlikely to have much effect, because several forms, such as *Nymphaea* spp., for example, establish large rhizomes buried in the substrate. These will be resistant to, and protected from, desiccation when the substrate is exposed by a fall in water level.

4. Submerged aquatic plants. These are also destroyed by desiccation when exposed to the air for prolonged periods, though the rate at which this occurs again depends on the ambient climatic conditions and, to some extent, on the thickness of the vegetation mass. Under certain circumstances, the dried outer layers of plant material form an insulation for the plants underneath them. When this occurs, the outer layers should be broken off in some way, if total destruction is required. Perennation by rhizomes submerged in the substrate is also a factor which can bring about rapid recovery of a population of submerged plants that may appear to have been totally destroyed after exposure to the air.

5. *Floating aquatic weeds.* These are the least sensitive to fluctuation in water level, except when it is rapidly lowered for a considerable distance, or when the plants are blown on to a shore from which the water is receding. Thus, when the level of Lake Kariba was lowered about 7 m in four months at the end of 1963 and beginning of 1964, large quantities of *Salvinia* were left stranded on the lake shore and, as a result, there was a probable reduction of approximately 250 km^2 in the extent of the *Salvinia* mats on the lake. Similarly large quantities of *Salvinia* are annually deposited on windward shores as the water recedes on the Chobe flood plains, Botswana, after the Zambezi floods. Mitchell & Thomas (1972) noted that this also appeared to be the regular pattern of events for floating vegetation in the areas flooded by rivers such as the Paraná and Amazon in South America.

5.2.5 *Light*

Because of their dependence on light for growth, submerged aquatic plants may be eliminated by decreasing the penetration of light to the depths at which they are growing. A cover of floating plants, which it may be possible to eliminate at a later date, or dense growths of algae in nutrient-rich waters, are both possible methods of achieving this but only if these plants would not pose problems by their own presence. Behrendt (personal communication) shades weeded areas by large sheets of black polythene which are just sunk over submerged plant growths, and descend to the bottom as the plants die. Fishing pitches could be cleared, or kept clear, in this way. The sheets may be transferred after a few months when the plants have been killed, or can be left, but must be moved before silt starts to accumulate. A slightly different technique is described by Templeton (1972).

5.2.6 *Wind, water currents and anchorage*

Because floating vegetation is independent of depth, changes in water level usually have little effect, and these plants are more sensitive to the effects of wind and water current. The plants will drift under the influence of wind until they fetch up against some form of projection above the water surface, which can serve as an anchorage. Plants accumulate and multiply in these situations and may build up large populations of nuisance proportions. Thus it is important to eliminate possible forms of anchorage for the plants in areas where it is desired to avoid the build-up of large floating mats.

The sensitivity of these floating plants to water currents provides a means for controlling them, where it is possible to manipulate this factor. Thus floating-weed problems can be minimized, if not prevented, by ensuring that water periodically moves along all canals. Floating-weed problems in this situation only appear to develop in undrained canals, which have been disused for long periods. Once the floating mats have stabilized, it is unlikely that the normal currents will be sufficient to move them and it will be necessary to resort to other methods.

5.2.7 *Biological interactions*

A further environmental factor which is open to manipulation is to utilize the knowledge that different biotic components of the system compete with one another for environmental resources. Shading out of submerged plants by plants above them is an example of this. However, other interactions between biological components are best considered under biological control and readers are referred to Chapter 6.

5.2.8 *Integration of control measures*

Aquatic plants in general may have to be dealt with by an integrated approach involving the manipulation of several environmental factors, together with conventional methods of chemical and mechanical control. The programme of mosquito control adopted by the Tennessee Valley Authority in its reservoirs is a good example of such an integrated approach to a problem of biological origin in an aquatic system (see also Chapter 6). Such a programme can only be formulated when there is sufficient information about the responses of the biotic components of the system to other environmental factors and the interrelationships between all of these during all seasons of the year. Unfortunately, in most cases, this situation is far from being realized. However, the possibility of constructing computerized models of aquatic ecosystems may provide a powerful tool for predicting the response of the system to events such as a fall in water level. Initially these models could be based on morphometric and other information available for the system under examination and also utilize information gained from similar systems. Obviously the first model constructed on this basis will be very approximate but analysis of such a model may often clearly indicate where more detailed information is required in order to achieve satisfactory simulation of the real system. Once this has been realized, the model can be used as a valuable aid in predicting the outcome of any changes in either the components of the system or its driving forces. In this way, ecosystem modelling may play a most important part in formulating rational management and research programmes. Furthermore, as information is acquired it is used to refine the model and thus improve its quality and accuracy of prediction.

5.3 RECOMMENDED PROCEDURES PRIOR TO CONSTRUCTION OF MAN-MADE WATER BODIES

5.3.1. *Introduction*

Man-made water bodies fall into two main types; *man-made lakes,* which are standing water bodies usually constructed by damming a river; and *canals,* which potentially contain moving water and are now usually constructed in connexion with irrigation schemes, though large canals have been constructed for transport.

Man-made lakes and systems of irrigation canals are generally difficult to modify after they have been constructed. Thus most of the measures to alleviate weed problems must be incorporated from the outset. However, the additional expense may be difficult to justify in the absence of accurate predictions about aquatic weeds in the proposed water body. The problem, and the challenge, to be faced by botanists is to evolve better methods of prediction for these phenomena.

5.3.2 *Man-made lakes*

Man-made lakes have recently been the focus of considerable multidisciplinary attention and, between 1965 and 1971, three international symposia (London, Accra,
Knoxville) have been held on this subject (Lowe-McConnel, 1966; Obeng, 1969,
AGU, in press). In addition, Neel (1963) has described the impact of reservoirs on
the limnology of North America, and the role of reservoirs in the management of
fishery resources was discussed at a symposium in the United States (American
Fisheries Society). Furthermore, Lagler (1969) has edited a publication of the Food
and Agriculture Organization of the United Nations on the planning and development of man-made lakes. In this, the effects and problems that occur as a result of
reservoir construction are set out, together with suggested procedures whereby these
problems could be minimized and the advantages optimized. Finally, in the second
report of the Scientific Committee on Problems of the Environment (SCOPE) of the
International Council of Scientific Unions (ICSU), Dussart, Lagler, Larkin, Scudder,
Szesztay and White (1972) discussed and reviewed the impact of man-made lakes on
the existing terrestrial and riverine ecosystems. They stressed the importance of prior
planning and careful monitoring of changes which occur and pointed out the
necessity to develop predictive models of man-made lake ecosystems, as the basis of
rational management programmes. The problems of plant growth and aquatic weeds
are included in the publications listed above, either as symposia papers (Little, 1966,
1969; Boyd, 1967; Hall, Laing, Hossain & Lawson, 1969; Mahal, 1969; Chapman,
Hill, Carr & Brown, in press; Martin, Bradford & Kennedy, in press; Mitchell, in press
a), or as comments and recommendations for action.

1. Pre-impoundment surveys. Pre-impoundment surveys of the proposed lake's
catchment for aquatic plants which could cause problems were advocated by Lagler
(1969) and Mitchell (in press *a*), while Edwards & Ne! (1972) gave a brief report on
such a reconnaisance survey in the catchment of the Hendrik Verwoerd Dam in
South Africa. The difficulty about such a survey is that the majority of sites visited
will be ecologically quite unlike those that will occur in the lake. Thus, it may be
necessary to go to some trouble to visit quiet backwaters and other areas of calm
water. Furthermore, because of these differences in habitat, the plants which are
potentially troublesome may be present in only very small quantities. For example,
Salvinia had not been observed in the Middle Zambezi Valley before impoundment of
Lake Kariba, though it was probably present in the flood plains of the Chobe River
above the Victoria Falls. Similarly *Eichhornia crassipes* was present in only four small
localities in the northern part of the basin of Lake Brokopondo, though, before
closure, small groups of the weed could always be observed in a few places on the
river banks above the lake (van Donselaar, 1968). Pre-impoundment catchment
surveys must therefore be concentrated on the careful examination of sites with the
most lacustrine conditions and pay particular attention to plant species that are
known to have caused weed problems or those that are ecologically similar. For
example, the water fern *Azolla nilotica,* which occurs on the east of Africa, has not
been known to cause weed problems and is mostly found in transitory pools, which it
rapidly covers during the growing season. However, it occurs in the catchment of the
Cabora Bassa Reservoir, which is now under construction on the Zambezi River in
Mozambique. When the reservoir fills the plant may be exposed to conditions it is
adapted to exploit but, this time, on a permanent rather than transitory basis.

Particular attention must be paid to floating plants as, initially, they are likely to
cause the most serious problems because of their independence of the large-scale

changes in water level that occur during the filling of a lake basin. Furthermore, plants which are not native to the area, such as *Azolla filiculoides* in the Hendrik Verwoerd Dam catchment (Edwards & Nel, 1972), must be viewed with grave suspicion because of the ability of many invading plants to grow explosively (see Chapter 3). Thus, when such a plant is known to occur in the vicinity of a proposed project but is not known from the catchment, it may be desirable to attempt to control its entry by attacking it in the known locality, even if it is not regarded as a nuisance there. The introduction of stringent quarantine precautions may also reduce the risk of accidental or deliberate importation into the free area. Such measures must include education of the public on the identification and disadvantages of the plant, inspection of boats and other equipment entering the weed-free area and the legislation to give power to those actions. Such a campaign instituted in 1961, together with constant vigilence have, so far, prevented the spread of *Salvinia* from Lake Kariba to other major man-made lakes in Rhodesia.

2. Shoreline features. Shoreline features have implications to all life forms of aquatic plants and, therefore, an essential aspect of pre-impoundment studies is the prediction of shoreline slope and its degree of protection from wind and wave action, through all ranges of predicted water level. Steep exposed shores are the least hospitable for plant growth, especially when rapid and extensive lake level fluctuations are superimposed on them. Furthermore, the area of suitable habitat is much less than on shallow shelving shores. For example, steep shorelines on Lake Kariba have little aquatic plant growth, both of submerged and floating species, even in sheltered areas, and emergent species are generally absent.

Shallow shorelines over which there is rapid, extensive lake-level fluctuations are generally inhospitable for aquatic plants but, after exposure by a receding lake level, they may be rapidly covered by terrestrial or wetland species. When these are tolerant of some degree of submergence, as is *Panicum repens* in Lake Kariba, they may become permanently established over considerable areas. Below the water, shallow shores are, generally, soon occupied by extensive growths of submerged species, especially where water is clear and light is transmitted to considerable depths. Large mats of floating species may develop in sheltered, shallow shoreline areas, which support 'woodland' of drowned trees projecting above the water surface. At one stage such partially submerged woodland was a favoured habitat for *Salvinia* on Lake Kariba (Mitchell, 1970) and for *Eichhornia crassipes* on Lake Brokopondo (van Donselaar, 1968). Judicious bush clearing of such areas will undoubtedly reduce floating weeds, though this may allow submerged weed beds to develop. The contrast between uncleared areas supporting floating weed mats and cleared areas infested with submerged plants can be clearly seen on Lake Kariba. Areas of shoreline have been cleared for fishing pitches on several lakes (e.g. Kainji, Kariba) and the policy is now the subject of some discussion (see Dussart *et al.*, 1972). However, it is clear that the decision whether or not to clear bush from the future lake bottom (and, if so, what form the clearing should take), must also take into account the predicted behaviour of aquatic weed populations.

Because troublesome weed growths are more likely on shallow shelving shorelines, it may be desirable to attempt to minimize their extent by designing a dam to impound water to a suitable level. However, shallow areas are likely to be the most biologically productive and, if any aspect of biological productivity, such as fisheries, is desired in the impoundment, these areas should be retained, in spite of the risk of aquatic weed problems, for which other contingency plans must be prepared.

3. Project design features. Other design features should also be considered in man-made lakes where floating aquatic weeds have been predicted. An adjustable surface spillway could be utilized to eliminate weed masses that are blown against the dam wall. This may be important when prevailing winds blow towards the lake outlet, as hydro-electric and other installations, which could be adversely affected by masses of floating weed, will be in this vicinity. In any case, care should always be taken in siting lake installations where they are least likely to be adversely affected by aquatic weed problems. Where a high nutrient status has been predicted for a proposed reservoir, the incorporation of multilevel outlets should also be considered. These could be used to draw off water from nutrient-rich lake strata, thus alleviating problems caused by aquatic weeds or plankton blooms.

5.3.3 Canals

Man-made water bodies, in which there is moving water, have to contend with rather different aquatic weed problems. Floating weeds are less likely to cause difficulties provided there is a sufficiently strong flow to carry the plants away and provided this occurs sufficiently often to prevent foci of infestation from building up into channel-wide blockages, which cannot then be moved. Such flows must of course be coupled with some method of removing the plants that are continuously being produced. This would be relatively simple to achieve with a boom or net across the end of the canal, which should be regularly cleaned. However, if the numbers of plants were allowed to develop to excessive amounts, such a system could rapidly become ineffective.

Submerged and emergent weeds are much more difficult to deal with and, in practice, provide the major problems in this type of installation. Because irrigation canals are relative shallow, light is usually sufficient for plant growth at all depths and, providing the substratum is suitable, luxurious growths of attached plants may soon develop. These cannot be moved by water flowing through the canal and can markedly reduce the efficiency of the system (see Chapter 4). Canals can be made less suitable for plant growth by making the substratum less suitable and/or by preventing the entry of light by covering with appropriate material, such as sheets of black polythene. Both features would be included if piping were used to transport water. However the costs of instituting such measures would have to be justified by the increased efficiency of the system and would also have to be shown to be less than other methods of control. Furthermore, experience has shown that the efficiency of piping and concrete-lined canals can be severely reduced by growths of fungi and bacteria in the dark and algae in the light. Usually such growths can be contained by careful chlorination of the water.

5.4 RECOMMENDED PROCEDURES FOR DEALING WITH AQUATIC WEED PROBLEMS

An aquatic weed problem may be actual or potential. The former is represented by the presence of an excessive population of aquatic plants, which can clearly be regarded as weeds in terms of the definition in Chapter 1. However, it is more difficult, but frequently more crucial, to be able to recognize a *potential* problem in time to contain it by relatively inexpensive means. Aquatic weeds frequently show an exponential growth pattern (Fig. 5) and thus may be much easier to contain when the plants are present in only small numbers. When numbers are high, the same

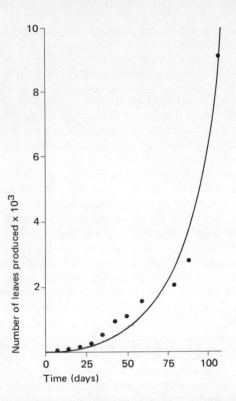

Figure 5. An exponential growth curve for *Salvinia molesta* recorded from a population of plants growing in a large box in a greenhouse from early winter to spring. Growth was recorded as increase in leaf numbers. Additional plant nutrients were supplied eighty days after the start of the experiment. Measurements did not continue but growth was eventually limited by the area of water available.

doubling time that was present from the outset may produce plants at a rate that will be impossible to deal with. The expense of the operation in the initial part of the growth curve is also likely to be less, though, to some extent, this depends on the dispersion of the plants. In most cases, there is a stage in the pattern of growth when an attack on the problem by a certain means is likely to be most efficient in terms of expense and effectiveness. However this stage may be different for different methods of control. Thus, manual control may be efficient and feasible at an early stage, whereas chemical control may be most efficient though more expensive at a later stage, when manual control is impracticable. Generally however, attempts at controlling the plants at an early stage by the least drastic methods are more favourable ecologically and economically.

5.4.1 *Potential aquatic weed problems*

There is no sure way to recognize a potential problem, just as it is difficult to predict with certainty a weed problem in a man-made water body prior to its construction. However, the same indications may be sought, namely: (a) the presence of an aquatic plant species, which has been known to cause problems in situations similar to those that exist in the threatened lake or river; (b) the presence of suitable habitats for the plant, or plants, to exploit; (c) the presence of an aquatic plant which is not native to the area.

Once a potential problem has been diagnosed, it is essential that the weed's growth and dispersion be carefully monitored, while possible methods of handling the problem are being investigated and evaluated. It is important to know, as accurately as possible, the present distribution of the plant, its method and rate of reproduction and the rate at which it is advancing. If the ecology and biology of the plant species happens to be relatively little known, then it is highly desirable that autecological studies be commenced as soon as possible. Even if the plant is one which had been studied in similar situations, but is invading a new environment for the first time, observations on its behaviour in the new situation will also be required. Possible methods of control should be considered and evaluated without delay. This will ensure that the best methods are known and available, if and when the decision is taken to carry out control measures against the plant. Such a programme requires ready capital and, as lengthy delays may have very expensive repercussions if the weed growth becomes unmanageable, it is economically wise to include contingency items for such investigations in the initial estimates for all man-made water resource constructions. This is particularly important in tropical regions where plant growth is likely to be very rapid and a potential problem quickly becomes an actual one.

5.4.2   Actual aquatic weed problems

An actual weed problem may necessitate short-term control measures using the best methods available to ameliorate cases of hardship in particular localities. However, unless the situation can be shown to be urgent, it may be desirable to carry out a detailed assessment of the problem and the methods of dealing with it before mounting wide-scale control measures, which may later be shown to be inefficient and even disadvantageous. For example, if the area of *Salvinia* on Lake Kariba had not been so large (approximately $1,000\ km^2$) and the cost of chemical control therefore prohibitive, it is possible that a campaign to control the weed would have been undertaken. Subsequently, it has been shown that the plant is valuable as a trap for nutrients (Mitchell, 1965) and as a habitat for invertebrates (Bowmaker, 1968) and widespread control could have had detrimental effects on the biological productivity of the system.

The detailed assessment of an actual weed problem should include the same type of procedures as for a potential one. The extent of the problem should be carefully assessed. If the area is large, aerial surveys using methods described in Chapter 3 coupled with confirmatory ground-level observations may be the most efficient method of obtaining an accurate record of the distribution and extent of the problem (van Donselaar, 1968; Mitchell, 1970). Autecological studies of the plant should be commenced as soon as possible and should include its relationship and effects on the environment in question and its methods and rates of reproduction and dispersal. The phenology and nutrition of the weed will also be important in providing information on which predictions of its future behaviour could be based. Finally, control measures of all types should be investigated and evaluated in economic terms and in relation to the ecological impact of each of the proposed methods.

The decision to apply control mesaures, no matter at what stage it is taken, should be based on quantified estimates, wherever possible. Furthermore, as many alternatives as possible should be available for consideration, including an assessment of taking no action. The possibility of environmental manipulation based on ecological knowledge of the weed species and of the environment should be considered as well as other more conventional methods of control. Generally the expense of control measures should be covered by the economic benefit of a reduced weed problem, though, in some cases, a strict evaluation on solely economic grounds can be dangerously misleading.

6. The control of aquatic weeds

6.1. Mechanical control

T. O. Robson,
Weed Research Organisation Begbroke Hill,
Yarnton, Oxford (United Kingdom)

The physical removal of plants obstructing flow or interfering with the use of a watercourse or lake is the simple direct approach to tackling the problems of aquatic weeds. It has been used traditionally wherever these problems occur and in most places has involved regular cutting at intervals throughout the growing season. In situations where this has been happening over long periods of time as in the case of Europe where it has been done annually for centuries, the fresh-water biological system has become adapted to it. It then forms part of the environment and is essential for the maintenance of the ecosystem.

Weeds are normally removed in two ways; cutting or dredging.

Depending upon the efficiency of the tools used, rooted submerged weeds are usually cut at a point near the base of the stem leaving the roots and rhizomes undisturbed. Dredging on the other hand removes a proportion of the buried parts of the plants in the mud from the bottom. It is a much slower and more costly operation than cutting and is usually used as a last resort to reclaim silted channels and lakes.

Being wholly controlled by man, both cutting and dredging permit him to exert the maximum control over the amount of weed removed within the limitations of the machine used, in contrast to the indirect and less determinate effects of herbicides and biological control agents. Because of this, cutting especially, has certain advantages over these other methods of weed control. Also cutting and removal of the plant material has the advantage of providing an opportunity for the utilization of the vegetation (see Chapter 7).

6.1.1 CUTTING

Submerged weeds

In many situations where fishing is important some macrophytic growth is needed to provide shelter for fish fry and invertebrate animals, to create conditions suitable for spawning and to replenish dissolved oxygen supplies. The management of fisheries in these circumstances requires the selective clearance of weeds either according to species of plant or to area occupied by the weed. In the highly sought-after trout streams of Europe and elsewhere, this has developed to a degree bordering on superstition and requires not only the careful use of hand-held tools, but also men trained in their use and steeped in the traditions of river management. The weed is cut precisely and with great care, and only those patches of weed felt to be surplus to the requirements of the stream are removed. The cost in labour for this work limits its application to those rivers where either labour is cheap or the benefits obtained from fishing justify it. Only by cutting can this type of weed management be possible.

It is unlikely that such precision is essential even in trout streams, and in most places the majority of the weed is cut at intervals throughout the growing season. The plant communities are adapted to this regular annual treatment and rapidly regrow until they reach the height at which they have to be cut again. The interval between cuttings varies with growing conditions and species, but in temperate zones during the summer it is usually no more than four weeks. The communities established under this type of management are dependent upon it continuing. The introduction of another technique that may increase the period of defoliation or the length of time between treatment and regrowth will alter the ecosystem and if this change is undesirable, regular cutting will have to continue.

Another advantage of cutting is that the result is predictable, whereas this is not always so with other methods because local conditions may bring about side effects, such as deoxygenation. Deoxygenation is caused primarily by the increased uptake of oxygen through the bacterial activity required to break down dead plant material. This is largely avoided when the cut material is removed from the water soon after cutting.

Emergent weeds

Emergent weeds growing in the water are cut at the same time as submerged weeds and regrowth is usually rapid. When flood prevention is the reason for weed control, plants growing on at least the lower part of the banks must also be cut. In certain circumstances wild-fowl and other wild-life interests are involved and it may be necessary to regulate the weed-control operation to avoid interfering with them at some vulnerable stage in their annual cycle, e.g. nesting period. This can best be controlled by adopting a cutting programme that will check the weed growth during periods of flood risk and allow it to regrow and provide the conditions suitable for wild-life at other times. In practice it does not always follow that these two requirements can be separated in this way, but when it is possible cutting allows the flexibility necessary to adapt management to meet the needs of both.

Some of the emergent plants such as *Phragmites australis* and the rushes (*Juncus* spp.) have been used traditionally for thatching, floor coverings, basket-making, etc., but in many instances these crafts are dying out as modern alternatives are found to be easier to obtain and equally suitable. For instance, at one time to supplement their wages men cutting reeds in drainage ditches in parts of Britain would carefully bundle them up for sale for thatching. This is no longer done because many of the old thatched cottages are being reroofed with more durable materials and the diminishing thatch requirements are being met from other sources.

Considerable attention has been given recently to the possibility of using submerged and floating weeds for animal feed or compost and this is discussed in detail in Chapter 7. A number of problems have to be overcome to make this a practical proposition but only by cutting will it be possible to achieve it at all.

The main disadvantages of cutting are more apparent in the industrialized countries where alternative well-paid work is available in industry for the men who would otherwise have been employed on aquatic weed control. Because weed regrowth is so rapid after cutting it is a continuous operation and labour and machines have to be tied up for the whole of the growing season on what is a purely maintenance task. The scarcity of labour and its increasing cost are forcing the adoption of labour-saving methods. Mechanization is partly an answer, but it does not overcome the need for continuous operations and measures that give long-term growth control are also being sought.

The stage of growth at which the plant is cut affects the rate of regrowth. For instance, working with *Phragmites australis,* Haslam found that cutting during the early emergence period (April/May in the United Kingdom) gives a full replacement crop while cutting later after the emergence period of new shoots is over (July in Britain) the replacement crop is negligible (Haslam, 1968). Defoliation soon after the end of the emergence period also prevents the replenishment of reserves (used in the emergence period) and affects the production of rhizomes. Cutting at later times has progressively less effect and by the time the aerial shoots are dying naturally their removal has no deleterious effect on the plant or regrowth at the beginning of the next season. These findings may also apply to other plants with similar seasonal growth regimes although Barrett & Robson (1971) found little evidence of this in their work on *Typha angustifolia* and *Glyceria maxima* and only a 30 per cent reduction in regrowth the following spring with *Carex riparia*. Some interesting current research (1972) at the Haryana Agricultural University, Hissar, India on *Typha* sp. (*T. angustata* or *T. domingensis*) indicates that submergence following cutting for four weeks or longer inhibits regrowth. This may have practical application in situations where water levels can be regulated and arranged to coincide with the optimum cutting period. Very little scientific research has been directed towards improving the levels of weed control achieved by cutting. The results of the work mentioned above demonstrate how studies of this kind can improve its effectiveness on emergent plants. Similar work on submerged plants may be equally rewarding. The main aspects likely to provide useful practical information are the timing of a cut in relation to the stage of growth of the plants, the degree of defoliation achieved and the frequency of and length of time between cuts. At the University of Wisconsin deep cutting of submerged weeds reduces regrowth (Livermore & Wunderlich, 1969) and Robson (1967) made a similar observation is his report of the problem of aquatic weeds in the United Kingdom.

The need to remove the cut material from the water and the need to dispose of it in some way makes cutting a double task with, again, a high labour requirement. The idea of offsetting these costs by finding some way of utilizing the plant material is the main impetus for the development of harvesters and drying equipment which is being attempted in the United States of America (Livermore & Wunderlich, 1969).

6.1.2   DREDGING

Dredging is seldom used solely for the purpose of controlling weeds but is brought in to remove silt, to deepen and to reshape watercourses and lakes. Much of the silting is a consequence of weed growth or has been hastened by it and further increases in the density of the plant populations follow the deposition of silt. Regular weed control by cutting or other methods can delay the need to use the dredgers or excavators.

A dredging operation involves the removel of most of the plant material together with some of the bottom mud and its deposition on the bank. Much of the stem and leaf growth of the plants is taken out in this way and,depending upon the depth of the new cut, a certain amount of root and rhizome as well. However, this is seldom done to the extent that all seeds, tubers and other plant propagules are removed and regrowth is, therefore, still possible. In drainage ditches in the United Kingdom the result usually is a more diverse population of macrophytes and in lakes and ponds dredging is often followed by an invasion of floating filamentous algae.

The main disadvantages of dredging are its cost in both time and money. If an excavator is used it also requires access along the whole length of a channel bank and suitable areas for the disposal of the spoil (mud and plant material). Because it is slow and expensive it is only used when the channel or lake has deteriorated severely and other forms of maintenance are no longer effective.

6.1.3 MACHINERY USED FOR WATER-WEED CONTROL

The implements and machines at present in use for the control of aquatic weeds have in most cases been developed to meet a local need by the operators themselves. As a result a range of tools differing widely in shape and performance has come into being and has been until comparatively recently handed down from generation to generation often with little modification. In the more developed countries the increasing difficulty of obtaining labour and its growing cost make the use of the traditional hand-held tools uneconomical and mechanized systems are being sought. However, in the developing countries manual methods of water-weed control are likely to persist and prove to be the most economical for the smaller channels while labour remains plentiful. For this reason some of the more successful of the manual operations are briefly described here, although they may not strictly fall into the category of machinery.

Where attempts have been made to mechanize weed cutting it has been found necessary to develop a range of tools to deal with the different situations encountered. Small hand-held machines are needed for the smaller channels inaccessible to boats or tractors. Narrow channels can often be managed from the bank and boats of one sort or another are needed for major canals and lakes. The growth-habit of the weed also affects the selection of the right tool; for example, a cutter designed for submerged weed control will be of little use against free-floating plants such as *Eichhornia crassipes*. It is not possible because of the diversity of the machines and tools available to provide a fully comprehensive list of machinery, but the most important items will be included and used to illustrate the principles involved.

1. Hand-held tools

The traditional tools used for centuries in Europe for water-weed control have evolved from implements used originally for agricultural purposes.

The scythe. With its sharp, horizontal 0.6 to 1.0 m long blade and its long wooden handle set at roughly right angles to the blade, the scythe was perhaps the most successful of these. Its handle has been modified a little but it is virtually the same tool as used in Europe for centuries to cut hay. Some skill is required to operate it, but once its use has been mastered, it is a very efficient means of cutting submerged weeds and can also be used for the grass and reeds on the bank. Although it is slow compared with the modern machines, in skilled hands it gives a closer cut and often results in slower regrowth. For this reason and also because it enables the operator to be selective in the weeds he removes, it is sometimes preferred to the faster, cheaper, but less precise, weed-cutting launches.

Sickles, grass hooks. Sickles and grass hooks with curved blades, and other tools used for cutting grass and weeds on dry land, are also used in water. Usually they are attached to longer handles so that the weeds on the bottom can be reached more easily.

Rakes and forks. Rakes and forks of various forms, with long handles and usually longer tines than normal, are useful for removing cut plant material and filamentous algae. They are also used from the bank to drag out submerged plants without cutting but a proportion of stems always remain behind and although they may be damaged regrowth is usually rapid. Forks have been used to lift floating plants of *Eichhornia crassipes* (water hyacinth) into barges in lakes, but this is a very slow operation and applicable only to small infestations or 'mopping up' after a major weed-control campaign.

Chain scythes and chain knives. These been developed to increase the rate at which weeds in channels up to about 6 m surface width can be cut. The crudest form of chain scythe is a series of scythe blades joined end to end by metal chain links with a length of rope attached to the last blade on each end. It is then operated by men working from both banks who pull it backwards and forwards across the bed of the channel as they slowly make their way along the watercourse. The weeds are thus cut near the base of their stems. For successful results the blades must be sharp and the sharpened edge facing the way the men are going. It is very heavy work and two or three men are needed on each bank to use it for any length of time. A lighter version consisting of numerous small serrated blades attached to a chain in such a way that a cutting edge is always facing the direction of cut is primarily used by fishermen in rivers and lakes. It is much easier to handle and to operate.

Mechanical. To overcome the problems of labour shortage while retaining some of the advantages of the traditional manual methods of weed cutting, attempts have been made to produce machines which simulate the performance of the ancient tools, but increase the output per man. This has been done primarily by mechanizing the cutting blade and introducing reciprocating cutters. One example of this is the 'mechanical scythe' in which the knife is driven by compressed air provided by a small mobile compressor unit capable of serving up to about six scythes. While it does speed up the cutting operations there are certain obvious disadvantages. First, it must be possible to keep the compressor near the operators and this means that easy access must be available along the bank. There is also a considerable risk of accidents to the men handling the scythes and this is increased when a number of operators have to be restricted to a limited area by the need to use one compressor.

Another tool sometimes used for water weeds is a hedge-trimmer with a 0.6 m reciprocating blade attached to one end of a 2 m shaft and driven by a small petrol engine at the other end. When in operation it is slung from the shoulder and easily manipulated to cut weeds both on the bank and up to a depth of 0.6 m in the water. Being designed as a hedge-trimmer the cutter bar is most suitable for cutting stems up to 1 cm diameter and is not satisfactory for thick-stemmed plants such as *Typha latifolia*.

2. Floating machines

A number of boats and barges have been designed specifically to cut aquatic weeds and in more recent years attention has been given to the development of machinery for harvesting the plants and converting them into some useful product, e.g. animal feeding stuff or compost.

Weed-cutting boats
Cutting mechanism. The first weed-cutting boats were developed soon after the First World War and have been used extensively in Europe and elsewhere ever since. Most of these early boats used a V-shaped knife, with blades about 1.5 m long and some

with a serrated edge, which was lowered into the water behind a boat and pulled along the channel bottom (Fig. 6). Its efficiency depended largely upon its sharpness. In some models it was attached to a rigid shaft and thus held at a predetermined depth to avoid striking stones and other obstacles on the bottom which would blunt it. In these cases the knife was usually oscillated back and forth so that as the boat went forward the knife followed in a series of jerks. The forward speed was therefore faster and its cutting power improved. In other models the knife was attached to a chain so it followed the bottom and cut the weeds lower down, but it was essential that the channel be free of obstruction.

Probably the commonest cutting mechanism is the reciprocating cutter bar based on the tractor-operated farm mowers, but with the fingers replaced by triangular teeth of the same size as those on the knife. The cutters vary in length from one to four metres and are attached horizontally at their centre to a vertical shaft in the bows of the boat. They are then lowered to the required depth and in recent models the depth of cut can be controlled hydraulically while in operation. Sometimes a vertical knife is placed ahead of the shaft to cut through floating weeds and prevent them from holding back the boat. With some makes of launch, knives that work at an angle to and above the water surface are available for cutting reeds and brush on the lower parts of the banks (Fig. 7).

Another type of reciprocating cutter has been developed over recent years in the United Kingdom. It is U-shaped, vertical and has teeth cut into two spring steel bands one of which is stationary while the other moves backwards and forwards over it (Fig. 8). Its usual width is about 2.5 m at the bottom and 4 m at the top with 2.2 m sides. It can cut to a depth of about 1.3 m and can be tilted from side to side to clear vegetation from the banks. The drive and all adjustments of the depth and angle of cut are hydraulically controlled by moving one lever. The knife is easily detached from the arm and can be replaced by a rake which extends to a width of 4 m and is capable of lifting up to 300 kg of weed at a time and dumping it on the bank.

The reciprocating cutters are usually driven by either an inboard engine that also provides power to the propellers, or by a separate, small, petrol motor supplied specifically for this purpose. In some more recent models, such as the U-shaped knife mentioned above, hydraulic motors are used and are proving very satisfactory wherever maintenance standards are adequate.

The mechanical destruction of free floating weeds such as water hyacinth (*Eichhornia crassipies*) has been attempted in the United States of America and two of the more successful machines developed have been the 'sawboat' and the 'Kenny' crusher (Livermore & Wunderlich, 1969). The sawboat had a row of vertical cotton-gin saw blades spaced about 2.5 cm apart on a horizontal spindle in front of the boat. The saws were lowered to half their diameter into the water and rotated at 800 to 1,000 revolutions per minute shredding the floating mats of vegetation they encountered. They were successful against water hyacinth and also against the rooted alligator weed (*Alternanthera philoxeroides*) and were used for many years.

The 'Kenny' crusher lifted mats of floating weed out of the water on to a wide conveyor belt on a barge, dropped the plants between two large rollers which crushed them and then deposited the crushed material back into the water. This machine was also used regularly for many years and proved successful against water hyacinth and alligator weed. It is claimed that one of these machines could cover 81 ha per month (Livermore & Wunderlich, 1969). At the time these two machines were in service other machines using similar principles were developed in other parts of the United States. All of them returned the organic matter to the water and would therefore be

Figure 6. V-shaped knife. Note serrated edge of blade and paddle-wheel arrangement.

Figure 7. Cutting emergent weeds from a boat with an angled blade.

unacceptable where deoxygenation and other results of organic pollution have to be avoided.

Means of propulsion. When weed is cut it floats to the surface immediately and fouls conventional propellers. A number of alternative methods of propulsion have been developed primarily to overcome this difficulty.

One of the most efficient systems is the use of *paddle wheels* either placed in front of the bows, at the stern or on each side. The latest models for small weed-cutting boats are hydraulically driven with each wheel having its own motor so that its speed and direction can be varied independently of the other and as a result the boats are highly manœuvrable. One criticism is that this system may lack sufficient power for work at speed or against fast currents, but for lakes and sluggishly flowing water it is very efficient. Larger, more powerful, paddle wheels are used on the bigger water-weed harvesters.

A boat built in France uses twin horizontal helical (spiral) steel *propellers* (Fig. 9) at the stern which are driven by an inboard engine that can pass through mud, silt and thick vegatation without clogging. This form of propulsion provides considerable power and the boat can be used in fast-flowing rivers, but it is not suitable for the precise work that requires a high degree of manœuvrability at low speeds.

In the United States, *air propellers* powered by aircraft engines have been used for some time to drive flat-bottomed launches in weedy conditions. The propeller, which is similar to that of an aircraft, is placed in the stern with suitable protective guards and the boat can reach speeds of 50 km/h. This system is generally used on inspection craft and not often on weed-cutting boats, but it is being used on at least one water-weed harvester developed in the United States of America.

The choice of *fabric for the hulls* depends upon the circumstances in which the boat is to be used and the purpose for which it has been built. Steel is usually preferred but where the launch has to be moved frequently from water to water, reinforced, moulded fibre glass hulls have been found satisfactory.

Harvesters

The increased awareness of the dangers of pollution and the undesirable results of eutrophication have stimulated an interest in the harvesting and utilization of aquatic weeds. In some countries it has for a long time been obligatory by law to remove cut plant material from the water to prevent pollution, but no economic use has yet been found for this material. However, the methods used would be suitable for harvesting the plant material for processing in some way. Usually the cut material floats to the surface and is concentrated at a selected point by current or wind. It is then pulled out by long-handled rakes, draglines (cranes), forks, floating conveyors or specially designed rakes on boats. The floating conveyors that do not incorporate a cutting blade as well, have not proved very successful because the floating plant material has to be brought to them and there is little or no saving in time or labour compared with raking manually or using a dragline. Recently rakes have been produced for attachment to the hydraulic system of a weed-cutting launch. This can be attached in place of the U-shaped cutting blade in a similar way and as easily as implements are changed on an agricultural tractor. By means of the hydraulic lift this rake can collect the material together, lift it up and drop it on to the bank.

Larger and very much more complex harvesters have been developed in recent years, primarily in the United States of America. They vary in detail but are all basically a large barge on which is mounted a belt-type conveyor and a suitable cutting mechanism. In some cases the harvested material is collected on the cutting

Figure 8. U-shaped cutting blade operated hydraulically.

Figure 9. Close-up of a pair of helical propellers.

barge which can be as much as 21 m long, and in others it is passed on to a separate barge that carries it to the shore.

One of the major problems with harvesting aquatic weeds and processing them economically into some useful product is the need to handle and remove large quantities of unwanted water. Bruhn, Livermore & Aboaba (1971) working on this problem in the United States tried two methods of overcoming these difficulties. They have found that by squeezing out the water in presses on board the harvesting vessel 68 per cent of the weight is removed as liquid and the volume is reduced to 16 per cent of the original. Some of the organic matter is also lost and returned to the water but they claim that of the original plant material 90 per cent dry matter, 85 per cent crude protein, 60 per cent potassium and 80 per cent phosphorus is retained. They are also trying an alternative technique of 'fluidizing' the weeds and pumping the resulting liquid ashore for processing or for use as a fertilizer on crops.

Bruhn *et al.* (1971) also consider that if the product is to compete with similar agricultural products for animal feeds, harvesting rates must be increased. This would involve major modifications to the harvesting equipment because the main impediment to speed is the water resistance of the wide conveyor belt in the bows of the barges, and fresh ideas and designs would be needed to overcome this. Further development must, however, depend largely on the potential value of the harvested plants and this subject is discussed in the next chapter.

3. Machines operating from the bank

*Excavators.*The principal use of excavators is to reshape and deepen existing water courses that have become silted, or to dig new channels. Weed control is usually incidental to the main work. However, there are instances where they have been used with a specially designed rake to remove cut weed or thick mats of filamentous algae. The machine usually chosen for this work is the 'dragline'. It has a steel cable passing over a jib, in a similar way to a crane, to which is attached a 'bucket' or 'scoop', but with a further cable which does not pass over the jib fastened to the bucket in such a way that it can pull the bucket towards the body of the machine and fill it with mud. A skilled operator can throw the bucket out from the bank and reach much further than is possible with a hydraulic jib. However, a hydraulic jib is much more precise and useful for accurate excavations and selective dredging.

Weed-cutting bucket (Figs. 10, 11). The weed-cutting bucket has been specially designed for water-weed control. It consists of a series of curved vertically arranged bars connected at their top ends to a horizontal bar and spaced equally along its length. Another bar with a reciprocating cutter joins their lower ends and the whole 'bucket' is attached at the centre of its length to the hydraulic jib of an excavator. In operation the lower edge with the cutter bar is lowered parallel to the soil surface and carried forward towards the excavator by the jib, cutting the weeds on the way. The cut weeds are collected in the 'bucket', which does not retain the water and mud, and are lifted out and dumped on the bank. This tool has been found very useful for narrower drainage and irrigation channels but the watercourse must be accessible from the bank with few or no trees and other similar obstructions. Buckets are produced in various sizes up to 4 m long and the smaller, lighter versions can be used on wheeled tractors.

Rotary and flail mowers. Rotary and flail mowers attached to hydraulic arms are useful for cutting grass and reeds on banks of watercourses (Fig. 12). None has been

Figure 10. Weed-cutting bucket on the hydraulically operated jib of an excavator.

Figure 11. Close up of weed-cutting bucket.

Figure 12. Rotary cutting mechanism on hydraulically operated arm.

developed specifically for this purpose but those used on highway maintenance and which operate from a tractor are usually adequate for the smaller ditches.

Suction dredges. Large sludge pumps adapted to suck mud and weeds out of drainage channels are sometimes used for cleaning drainage ditches. The spoil is either spread over adjacent land or carried away in trucks.

Small mowers for vegetation control on banks. Many different kinds of small mowers are used on the steep banks of drainage and irrigation channels. The normal wheeled mowers with reciprocating cutter blades are difficult to use because of steepness of the slope. Rotary cutters, and especially those that do not have wheels but travel on a cushion of air, are better because they can be used up and down the slope instead of along it. Some special equipment has been developed in the Federal Republic of Germany and the Netherlands for use in areas of intensive cropping where there is no space at the top of the bank for tractors. Most of these have long reciprocating cutter bars operated from small tractors designed for market gardening and which require less than 0.6 m space for their wheels on the top of the bank.

6.1.4 THE FUTURE

The mechanization of water-weed control in the past has developed haphazardly with local engineers and others responsible for weed control adapting agricultural, dredging and other machinery to their needs and sometimes inventing and building tools to overcome a particular local problem. Since the Second World War there has been more commercial interest and this has resulted in specialized boats and barges for cutting and harvesting aquatic plants. The development of new machines or the modification and improvement of existing equipment depends on further investment of capital which will only be made if adequate returns can be expected. Much will depend on finding profitable uses for the harvested material and economic methods of handling and processing it. Impetus will also come from the need to avoid excessive eutrophication and pollution and, in certain highly populated countries, from the need for animal food. But the final decisions must be based on economics and the advantages of mechnical harvesting compared with harvesting through fish and other animals or establishing long-term weed control by herbicide use.

6.2. Chemical control

Robert D. Blackburn.,
United States Department of Agriculture, Agricultural Research Service,
Fort Lauderdale, Florida (United States of America)

6.2.1 INTRODUCTION

Aquatic weeds and algae in ponds, lakes, streams and canals present many and varied problems for persons using such bodies of water. Excess growth of aquatic plants obstructs water flow, increases evaporation, interferes with navigation, prevents fishing and other recreational activities, destroys wild-life habitats, lowers real-estate values, and presents health hazards. Aquatic weeds also are shortening the life span of our waters by increasing organic debris and accumulating sediment, thus accelerating the ageing process (Mackenthum, Ingram & Porges, 1950). The concept of aquatic weed control must be considered differently in the management programme in ponds, lakes and streams. A certain amount of aquatic vegetation in a given body of water is necessary for fish and waterfowl management, although no one has determined the optimum proportion of plant to water area (Bennett, G. W., 1962).

The control of aquatic nuisances should be first directed to the one basic cause: increased fertility of the aquatic environment. Uncontrolled drainage from heavily fertilized farmland, the discharge of untreated or partially and inadequately treated domestic and industrial wastes, the discharge of effluents from treatment plants, and drainage from garbage dumps all contribute nutrients to a body of water. To control nutrient levels we must practise pollution abatement. The problem is one of great magnitude and solutions for controlling nutrient levels will be slow in coming. Control of aquatic weeds, if only sometimes temporary, is necessary if man is to enjoy and utilize his water resources to the fullest extent.

The multiple use of water makes it very difficult to make general statements concerning control procedures with herbicides. The direct and indirect effects of applying herbicides to water must be considered at the time of treating each body of water.

6.2.2 BENEFITS OF USING HERBICIDES

In the United States of America, submerged weeds may be controlled with herbicides at one-fourth to one-third the cost of mechanical means (Harrison, Blackburn, Weldon, Orsenigo & Ryan, 1966). Research on biological methods has not progressed to the point where effective control measures are available. Large areas of aquatic plant infestations may be treated with aerial applications of herbicides. Granular formulations or low-volume sprays may be used to eliminate aquatic weeds and algae in small areas.

The concentration of most herbicides necessary to affect fish or other aquatic organisms is considerably higher than the amount necessary to control aquatic weeds. For example, 6,7-dihydrodipyrido [1,2-a:2',1'-c] pyrazinediium ion (diquat) has a threshold toxicity of about 20 p.p.m.w. for fish (Walker, 1963), which is approximately ten to twenty times the concentration necessary to inhibit plant growth.

Herbicide selectivity for aquatic weeds is limited. Some selectivity can be accomplished by the use of certain herbicides, by varying the concentration of chemical applied, by the application technique, or by the formulation of the herbicide.

Broadleaf aquatics usually are more susceptible to (2,4-dichlorophenoxy) acetic acid (2,4-D) than narrowleaf aquatic plants when treated at the same concentration. A low concentration of 2-chloro-4, 6-bis (ethylamino)-*s*-triazine (simazine) may effectively control algae but has no effect on higher aquatic plants.

The removal of one plant species from a group of morphologically similar species may be accomplished by the concentration of herbicide applied (Holm, Weldon & Blackburn, 1969). Giant duckweed (*Spirodela polyrhiza* (L.) Schleid.) is much more sensitive than watermeal (*Wolffia colombiana* Karst.) to diquat at a concentration of 0.1 p.p.m.w. but both species are killed by higher concentrations (Blackburn & Weldon, 1965).

Pre-emergence applications of some herbicides, such as (2, 3, 6-trichlorophenyl) acetic acid (fenac), make it possible to control the weed species before they become a problem, or to apply the chemical during a time when it will affect the aquatic environment least (Blackburn, 1966). During winter drawdowns, the herbicide can be applied to the soil to prevent the regrowth of the weeds when the water returns to normal depth.

Granular and pelleted formulations, and invert emulsions have made it possible to place the herbicide in closer contact with the aquatic weeds. Selective placement of the herbicide reduces drift and volatility, and injury to desired plants ; and it may increase effectiveness of the chemical on rooted aquatic plants.

Some of the herbicides used in the aquatic environment dissipate rapidly, leaving no residue. For example, the diquat which is not taken up by the treated plants is adsorbed on organic and clay materials (Blackburn & Weldon, 1962 ; Coats, Funderburk, Lawrence & Davis, 1966 ; Yeo, 1967). Seldom can diquat be detected in the water fourteen days after treatment. Another chemical, 7-oxabicyclo (2.2.1) heptane-2, 3-dicarboxylic acid (endothall), disappears rapidly from the aquatic environment (Hiltibran, 1962). Part of the removal from the aquatic environment may involve biodegradation.

The extensive use of aromatic solvents in the United States of America and of acrolein in both the United States of America and Australia has occurred despite their toxic effects on fish and other aquatic fauna. Research and extensive field use during the past twenty years with aromatic solvents and ten years with acrolein show they are not toxic to irrigated crops at concentrations required to control submerged aquatic weeds, or several times those concentrations (Timmons, Frank & Demint, 1969; USDA, 1963). In most of western United States of America, and apparently in Australia, canals and drains are not used as fisheries. The purpose of the irrigation and drainage systems is to deliver water to crops or drain excess water from land. Therefore, any fish killed in treated canals are considered expendable. However, this situation does not apply to most of California and Arizona, where the predominantly urban populations object to fish killed in any aquatic situation, including irrigation canals.

Aquatic plants can be controlled effectively with certain herbicides. However, because of the multiple use of the aquatic environment, the herbicides used will depend on the weed species involved, the area of infestation, and the immediate use of the water.

Figure 13.   The upper photograph shows the aerial spraying of a mixed stand of water hyacinth and water lettuce with 0.45/ha diquat; the lower photograph shows the area six weeks after application.

6.2.3 CONSEQUENCES OF USING HERBICIDES

When applying herbicides in the aquatic environment, one must consider the possible hazards to the user, to the consumer of the water or of the fish, and to vegetation, fish, wild-life and irrigation. Herbicides that damage the aquatic environment may be considered as poisonous, noxious or polluting materials. This may lead to arrests by pollution enforcement agencies at the county, state or federal level. It is essential, therefore, that the user of aquatic herbicides inform himself of the possible adverse effects of his aquatic weed control activities.

Herbicides used on the aquatic weeds enter water, and the risk of adverse side effects are greater than when the same herbicides are applied to terrestrial plants or soil. Instead of remaining on one crop or field, the herbicide may be moved by currents from place to place in a pond or lake, or for considerable distances if applied along or in a flowing stream. The removal of water from the treated area by man may result in the contamination of additional areas. This increases the risk of possible side effects from a single application of a herbicide. The complexity of using herbicides in water makes it very difficult for aquatic weed scientists to make generalized statements concerning control procedures.

The effect of the aquatic herbicide on humans must be considered carefully before application. Only one herbicide, copper, is cleared for use in potable water in the United States of America. The contamination of a water supply by the application of a herbicide not registered by a governmental agency might be hazardous to the people using the water. Frequently, it is difficult to predict what water will eventually be used for a potable purpose. The ambiguous term potable water as used by many states and governmental agencies can result in serious problems in connexion with herbicides.

Toxicity to mammals other than man should be given serious consideration before applying aquatic herbicides to water. Not only must the toxic effect of the herbicide on animals be considered, but also the possible contamination of consumable animal products such as meat, eggs and milk that may result from the animals drinking treated water.

Direct toxicity of a herbicide to fish should be known by the user. Even though the toxicity of a herbicide is known, the user must accept the responsibility if he makes a mistake and applies concentrations above safety levels. Long-term effects of many aquatic herbicides on fishes remain to be studied. Only recently have studies shown that certain aquatic herbicides may affect fish reproduction the year following treatment.

The indirect effect of aquatic herbicides may kill fish by a rapid drop in dissolved oxygen. Deoxygenation is the principal hazard to fish in the treatment of ponds, lakes and streams densely infested with weeds (Surber, 1961). The primary cause of oxygen depletion is the decomposing vegetation.

Herbicides also may kill planktonic algae, thereby reducing the fish food supply. Organisms that use the aquatic weeds for attachment, and which are part of the fish food supply, may be killed or driven from the treated area by the herbicide or decomposing vegetation. Scientists consider some aquatic plants as an essential part of the fishery environment.

Aquatic plants provide a large percentage of the diet of waterfowl. Removal of vegetation from a pond, lake or stream can result in the restricted use of the area by waterfowl.

The build-up of organic debris in the bottom of ponds, lakes, and streams from continuous herbicidal treatment is a matter of wide concern. The rate at which the debris accumulates is not known, but there is an accumulation after herbicidal treatment of dense weed infestations.

Sheffield (1967) has shown that certain aquatic plants may remove excess nutrients from the water. Mechanical harvesting of these plants may slow down the eutrophication process, thus lengthening the life of the aquatic environment.

The control of aquatic weeds in ponds, lakes, and streams is difficult, but a greater problem is how to avoid a clash between the various groups using the water. The conservationist usually wants the aquatic plant growths while others want the weeds removed so the water can be used for recreation and irrigation. The priority given one group over the other is a matter of local concern. A compromise solution may be sought by adopting an integrated programme of using herbicidal, mechanical and biological control methods.

6.2.4   HERBICIDES USED

Herbicidal treatment of aquatic weeds and algae is widely recommended in many areas of the world. Tremendous progress has been made in the last decade on control of aquatic weeds and algae with various inorganic and organic herbicides. Herbicides must pass rigid tests on efficacy, toxicity to fauna and flora in and near the waterway, persistence and other hazards before they can be used in the aquatic environment.

Aromatic solvents. Many herbicides and herbicidal combinations have been used for the control of aquatic weeds and only the most commonly used herbicides will be discussed here. However, particular plants and special circumstances may necessitate the investigation of a wide range of herbicides and herbicidal combinations. In such cases the weed control officer or the appropriate governmental agency should be contacted about the problem.

Experiments have been conducted to determine the tolerance of crops to aromatic solvents in irrigation water (Arle, 1950 ; Bruns & Dawson, 1959 ; Sutton, Weldon & Blackburn, 1970). These studies showed that water containing an aromatic solvent at concentrations recommended for submerged aquatic weed control in canals, about 1:3 l/l.sec during a period of 30 to 60 min, may be used for furrow or flood irrigation without injury to a wide variety of fifteen different crops. Extensive field experience during twenty years has corroborated those results and has shown that overhead sprinkler irrigation with water containing those concentrations of aromatic solvents caused no reported injury to crops.

Treated water is distasteful and livestock or wild-life refuse to drink it. Aromatic solvents have been used for many years in diversified farming areas, and no ill effects to animals drinking the treated water have ever been reported (Sutton, Weldon & Blackburn, 1970).

Water containing an aromatic solvent is very toxic to fish and many other aquatic organisms. Fish, crayfish, snails and various insects that come in contact with treated water are killed.

Aromatic solvents are highly volatile and are rapidly lost from the emulsion in flowing water. Monitoring tests showed that only 1 to 3 per cent of the chemical applied was found about 13 to 16 km downstream from the point where 575 p.p.m.w. was applied (Timmons, Frank & Demint, 1969).

Acrolein. This chemical is highly volatile and is very reactive with air and most organic substances. Hazards and losses of chemical are prevented by storing acrolein in high-pressure cylinders in which all air above the acrolein is replaced by nitrogen gas. The acrolein is introduced under water in canals and drains through plastic tubes under nitrogen gas pressure from auxiliary cylinders. Gas masks should be used by men who apply or otherwise handle acrolein to prevent severe discomfort to eyes and nasal passages if acrolein is accidentally released into the air.

Acrolein is highly toxic to fish, frogs, snails, crayfish and other aquatic fauna at 0.01 to 0.02 p.p.m.w., the lowest concentrations that will control submersed weeds during long exposure (Timmons, Frank & Demint, 1969). Therefore extreme care must be used to avoid emptying treated water from the lower end of an irrigation canal or drain into a small stream or pond. A much larger body of water is needed to dilute the concentration of acrolein quickly below that which is toxic to fish. Acrolein, like aromatic solvents, should be used only in canals and drains which are not used for fishing or where fish are considered less important than delivering water to or from crop land.

Farm animals have never been observed drinking acrolein-treated water, probably because of the disagreeable odour. In one investigation, lactating dairy cows were force-fed acrolein in drinking water at levels of 30 and 60 p.p.m. for 24 hours with no adverse effects on body weight, or milk or butterfat production. This shows a considerable safety margin over the maximum concentrations of 15 p.p.m. during 4 hours used for control of submerged weeds in small canals.

In early field experiments, furrow or flood irrigation with water containing maximum concentrations of acrolein varying from 20 to 60 p.p.m.w. did not reduce the yields of corn, cotton, or sugar beets (Bruns, Yeo & Arle, 1964). In a more recent experiment, acrolein applied at 0.1, 0.6 or 15 p.p.m.w. in 200 m^3 of water by furrow or sprinkler irrigation caused no yield reductions in corn, soybeans, or sugar beets. The sprinkler irrigation containing 15 p.p.m.w. of acrolein caused a slight, but temporary, injury of soybean and sugar-beet leaves. No injury to crops from extensive use of acrolein-treated water by farmers has been reported.

Amitrole-T. Amitrole-T has a wide range of safety to fish. Also, it has caused no injury to six different crops that were furrow irrigated at rates ranging from 0.25 to 4.5 kg/ha in several experiments (Bruns & Dawson, 1969). These rates gave concentrations from one-third to three times the highest concentrations of amitrole in water that have been found thus far in irrigation water following an application of amitrole to control bank weeds (Timmons, Frank & Demint, 1969). Amitrole, like dalapon, is registered in the United States for use only in drainage canals, but it has been used extensively many years for control of grass weeds and cat-tail along irrigation canals. Amitrole has been banned from use in or near water in England.

Copper sulphate. The first used, and probably the most economical chemical of all herbicides used in the aquatic environment, is copper sulphate pentahydrate (hereinafter referred to as CSP). This chemical was recommended for algae control in 1904 (Moore & Kellermann, 1904). Most species of algae may be controlled with a concentration of 1.0 p.p.m.w. of copper or less (Crance, 1963 ; Eipper, 1959; Seaman & Thomas, 1966 ; Smith, 1939; Snow, 1956). Some algae, i.e. *Pithophora* spp., are resistant to CSP and require high concentrations of copper, or repeated applications, or both. Applications of CSP at 112 to 560 kg/ha are necessary for control of some submerged species (Crance, 1963, Huckins, 1955 ; Huckins, 1960 ;

Ware, 1966). Most emerged species appear to be resistant to CSP (Sanders & Cope, 1966 ; Snow, 1963).

Susceptibility or resistance to CSP may be related to copper uptake. Variation in copper content has been found in several species of aquatic plants after treatment with CSP (Bon, Lewis & Fryer, 1960).

CSP is the only herbicide approved for potable water in the United States of America. From 1942 to 1962 the permissible concentration of copper in drinking water was 3.0 p.p.m.w. (anon., 1962). In 1962 the concentration was lowered to 1.0 p.p.m.w. because amounts higher than this affected the taste of water.

The effectiveness of CSP may be reduced in waters with a methyl orange alkalinity of 50 p.p.m.w. or more owing to precipitation of the copper by carbonates (Blackburn, 1966). Applications of CSP in a granular form may result in adsorption of copper by the hydrosoil with a subsequent loss of herbicidal activity (Toth & Riemer, 1968). However, in flowing water, copper sorbed by sediment may be slowly released back into the water over a period of many hours (Nelson, Bruns, Coutant & Carlile, 1969). CSP is toxic to fish and many invertebrates and care must be taken to avoid exceeding recommended doses in situations where these organisms are important.

Sodium arsenite. Another cheap and effective herbicide, $Na As O_2$ (sodium arsenite), is used for the control of submerged and floating aquatic weeds, but its toxicity to mammals and aquatic fauna greatly restricts its use. It has been used to control aquatic weeds in Wisconsin lakes since 1926 (Mackenthum, 1950). This is one of the first aquatic herbicides and is still used in some ponds and lakes. Recommendations vary from 4 to 8 p.p.m.w. for submerged weeds (Surber, 1943 and 1949) . In spite of its proven effectiveness under a wide range of conditions, it has always had the inherent drawback of toxicity to mammals (0.02 g may kill a man).

Most fish will withstand concentrations of sodium arsenite greater than that recommended for aquatic weed control. The question of possible build-up of arsenic in bottom muds and its effect on fish production has been studied. One study has shown adverse effects on pond life while another has shown no effect after ten years of use (Little, 1968). The use of sodium arsenite in the aquatic environment is now discouraged by most aquatic weed scientists. Danger of toxicity to the spray operator and wild-life has prompted this action. However, potable waters may contain up to 0.05 p.p.m.w. sodium arsenite.

Phenoxyd herbicides. The phenoxyd herbicide used most often in the aquatic environment is 2,4-D. It is used widely for controlling the growth of many submerged, emerged or floating weeds. The effectiveness of 2,4-D can be regulated by formulating it as an acid, sodium salt, amine salt or ester (Lawrence, 1962). The acid and salt forms increase the solubility while the heavy esters decrease its volatility. Broadleaf aquatic plants are very susceptible to 2,4-D. For example, 1.1 to 4.5 kg amine 2,4-D per ha are recommended for water hyacinth (*Eichhornia crassipes* Mart.) (Southern Weed Conference, 1960). Higher rates are required for narrowleaf and submerged plants.

Surfactants help to increase the penetration of 2,4-D after applications to emerged and floating weeds. The movement of 2,4-D in the plant is associated with translocation of assimilates in the phloem (Crafts, 1964). Direction of movement depends primarily on the placement of the chemical. In parrotfeather (*Myriophyllum brasiliense* Camb.), 2,4-D-1-^{14}C applied to mature leaves moved in a basipetal direction and was detected in the nutrient solution after four days, but no movement occurred after application to the roots or apical portion of the shoot (Sutton & Bingham, 1970).

Woody and other vegetation on the periphery of the aquatic environment can be more effectively controlled with (2,4,5-trichlorophenoxy) acetic acid (2,4,5-T) than with 2,4-D. Another herbicide, 2-(2,4,5-trichlorophenoxy) propionic acid (silvex fenoprop) is effective on certain aquatic plants. Some submerged weeds can be controlled with 0.5 to 2.5 p.p.m.w. silvex (Houser & Gaylor, 1969 ; Younger, 1958). A decrease in carbohydrate levels in floating alligator weed (*Alternanthera philoxeroides* (Mart.) Griseb.) indicated that 9 kg silvex/ha followed by a retreatment in two months is one of the most effective chemical control measures for this plant (Weldon & Blackburn, 1969).

Treatments with silvex at 2 p.p.m.w. were neither toxic nor inhibitory to growth of zooplankton in a farm pond (Cowell, 1965). Bluegill (*Lepomis macrochirus* Rafinesque) had a median tolerance limit (TLM) of 2.4 p.p.m.w. silvex in soft water for a 96-hour period; however, 7.2 p.p.m.w. was the TLM for fathead minnows (*Pimephales promelas* Rafinesque) (Surber & Pickering, 1962).

Endothall. Endothall is widely used for control of submerged weeds in the United States of America (Blackburn, 1966). It is not applied as the free acid but is converted to its inorganic or amine salts. The most active salts of endothall are: disodium, dipotassium, mono and di-(*N,N*-dimethyl alkylamine), and dihydroxy aluminium. The amine salt formulations control several types of algae.

The inorganic salts of endothall are safe to fish at concentrations of 100 to 800 p.p.m.w. (Keckemet, 1969). However, the long-chain amine salts are toxic to fish at concentrations of 0.2 to 1.0 p.p.m.w. (Walker, 1963). The amine salts are 2 to 3 times more active on aquatic weeds than the inorganic salts but 200 to 400 times more toxic to fish. Oysters and clams were not affected by rates of 5 to 10 p.p.m.w. of the inorganic salts. Experiments using the inorganic salts have shown a wide margin of safety to *Daphnia* spp. The various salts of endothall do not adversely affect other fish food organisms (Walker, 1963).

Entothall is a typical contact type, membrane-active, herbicide. Translocation in aquatics apparently is limited to the symplast (Thomas & Seaman, 1968). Endothall greatly accelerates protoplasmic rotation in elodea (*Elodea canadensis* Michx.) leaf cells. Research also has shown that elodea metabolizes endothall considerably faster than does American pondweed (*Potamogeton nodosus* Poir). This may explain relative resistance, of one species and relative susceptibility of another (Bon, Lewis & Fryer, 1960 ; Maestri, 1967 ; Seaman & Thomas, 1966 ; Thomas, 1966).

Endothall disappears completely from the soil in one to three weeks and from water one to ten days after application. This herbicide is considered highly biodegradable. Studies have shown that plants, fish and snails are capable of completely metabolizing endothall. It appears that the breakdown fractions of the herbicides are utilized by the biochemical systems of organisms and finally released in the form of carbon dioxide (Keckemet, 1969).

United States federal registrations prohibit the use of endothall in potable water. Treated water cannot be used for irrigation, agricultrual sprays, recreation or livestock watering within seven to twenty-five days after treatment, depending on the salt and concentration applied. Fish from treated areas should not be used for food or feed within three days after treatment. Endothall in water is prohibited in some European countries because of its mammalian toxicity.

Figure 14. A flood control at time of treatment (top) and the same canal two weeks after treatment with 3 p.p.m.w. of the amine salt of endothall for control of hydrilla (bottom).

Diquat. Diquat is a potent water-soluble herbicide with a relatively broad spectrum of activity on submerged and floating aquatic plants (White, 1962, 1965). Diquat has received considerable attention as an aquatic herbicide in the United States of America. (Blackburn & Weldon, 1963; Lawrence & Blackburn, 1963; Surber, 1961). It has been formulated as various salts, but it presently is marketed only as the dibromide salt. Both the herbicidal activity and the organic chemical reactions of diquat formulations are dependent solely upon the diquat cation and are not influenced by the nature of the associated anion.

Diquat usually is considered safe to use in the aquatic environment at recommended dosages. Applications in the field have not led directly to reduction in fish and wild-life populations.

Acute toxicity of diquat to fishes depends on the fish species and the hardness of the water (Bon, Lewis & Fryer, 1960 ; Gilderhus, 1967 ; Surber & Pickering, 1962). The TLM value ranges from 2.1 to 140 p.p.m.w. for a ninety-six hour period. Crosby & Tucker (1966) reported medium immobilization concentrations (IC_{50}) of 7.1 p.p.m.w. diquat for *Daphnia magna Straus*. Gilderhus (1967) found that 1 p.p.m.w. diquat prevented the formation of the adult stage of *Daphnia* spp. and that all stages were killed after exposure to 3 p.p.m.w. for eight days. Wilson and Bond (1969) reported the herbicide was 300 times more toxic to an amphipod (*Hyalella* spp.) than to a mayfly (*Callibaetis* spp.).

Diqaut is a contact herbicide which is very rapidly absorbed, or adsorbed, or both by foliage. Translocation has been noted via the xylem under certain conditions. Herbicidal action is dependent on the intensity of the incident light. The unique property of this herbicide is its very rapid and complete inactivation by soil. It is also bound by reaction with humic acid and adsorption on to organic matter (Coats, Funderburk, Lawrence & Davis, 1966). The persistence of diquat in water is related to these factors.

It has been theorized that certain soil microorganisms may degrade diquat, but studies with some vascular plants have indicated that this chemical is resistant to biodegradation processes (Funderburk & Lawrence, 1964). Diquat can be lost via photochemical decomposition (Funderburk, Negi & Lawrence, 1966). Federal regulations prohibit the use of diquat in potable waters in the United States of America. Water treated with diquat should not be used for human or animal consumption, swimming or irrigation within ten days after treatment. Recently, an interim tolerance of 0.01 p.p.m.w. has been proposed for residues of diquat in potable waters.

Paraquat. Paraquat has received considerable attention as an aquatic herbicide throughout the world. Research has shown little difference in the aquatic herbicidal activity of diquat and paraquat on floating and submerged aquatics, but paraquat is superior on emergent aquatic plants.

In the United States paraquat has not been registered for aquatic weed control while in many other areas of the world it is registered for use in aquatic sites. Paraquat has been shown to have a longer persistence in water (Coats, Funderburk, Lawrence and Davis, 1966).

Paraquat is safe to fish and wild-life at the rates recommended for aquatic weed control. The applicator of paraquat and diquat should avoid breathing spray mist or getting concentrate on skin. A repeated exposure of skin to paraquat may increase the ease of absorption.

Dalapon. Aquatic grasses and cat-tails (*Typha* spp.) are generally controlled with 2,2-dichloropropionic acid (dalapon). It is toxic to many grasses and other monocotyledons, but usually does not have any serious effect on broadleaf plants. Dalapon can be used at any stage of plant growth but is most effective on some perennial weeds when applied at flowering (Robson, 1968). During this time much of the dalapon is moved from the leaves to the roots and underground stems resulting in better control of regrowth. A combination of dalapon and emulsified diesel oil has been very effective on difficult and hard to-control species of cat-tail (Blackburn & Weldon, 1963).

Dalapon has a wide range of safety to fish and other aquatic life. No mortality to fish exposed to 100 p.p.m.w. was observed during a twenty-four-hour period. Dalapon usually breaks down in soil within six weeks. The persistence in water is about the same. It is broken down by microbial activity in the soil, but it is not degraded in the plant. It has caused no injury to crops irrigated with water containing twice the concentration found in water after application for control of bank weeds (Maestri, 1967).

Research has been carried out on combinations of other herbicides with dalapon. A combination of dalapon and trichloroacetic acid (TCA) is now marketed in many areas of the world. Dalapon is effective on hard-to-wet species when a surfactant is added to the spray solution.

Dichlobenil. A powerful inhibitor of germination and of actively dividing meristems is 2,6-dichlorobenzonitrile (dichlobenil). It is strongly adsorbed by seed coats and epidermis of shoots (Taylor, 1966). These properties give this herbicide a unique place in aquatic weed control. It is most effective when applied prior to active weed growth or when the weed species are dormant.

Figure 15. The dark square areas in the centre of the photograph are fragrant water lily treated six months earlier with an application of dichlobenil at 2.6 kg/ha.

Maximum water solubility of dichlobenil is 18 p.p.m.w. (Massini, 1961). It has a relatively high volatility when applied to a terrestrial soil. It has been used in aquatic sites as a pre-emergence herbicide in dry canals or pond bottoms where it has been necessary to incorporate the herbicide into the soil, or as a granular formulation applied over the water surface. Dichlobenil has been very effective on many species of aquatic weeds when applied to the exposed bottom of a lake, pond or stream. It has received wide publicity in the United States of America as a control for many species of water lilies (Taylor, 1968).

No adverse effects on wild-life have been noted. The toxicity of dichlobenil to several fish species is reported to have TLM values ranging from 10 to 23 p.p.m.w. (Van Valin, 1966). Walker (1964b) found that the formulation of dichlobenil affected its degree of toxicity to fish. Sanders and Cope (1966) reported immobilization EC_{50} values of 5.8 and 3.7 mg/dichlobenil for *Simocephalus* spp. and *Daphnia* spp., respectively. The herbicide is less toxic to amphipods than to aquatic insects (Wilson & Bond, 1969).

Triazines. Simazine is a promising herbicide of the triazine family for the control of aquatic weeds. Concentrations of simazine necessary to affect fish or other aquatic organisms are considerably higher than the amount required to inhibit plant growth (Walker, 1964a). Low concentrations of simazine, 0.5 to 2.0 p.p.m.w., are effective for the control of many algal species (Flanagan, 1966; Snow, 1963; Sutton, Evrard & Bingham, 1966); furthermore, higher amounts, 2.0 to 5.0 p.p.m.w., are necessary to control high aquatic plants (Blackburn, 1966 ; Sutton, Evrard & Chappel, 1965; Walker, 1964a). Submerged plants are more susceptible to simazine than emerged plants, but this may be due to the manner in which simazine is absorbed by the plant.

The toxic effect of simazine is due principally to its inhibition of the Hill reaction (Moreland, Gentner, Hilton & Hill, 1959), therefore simazine must enter the leaves. Simazine is readily absorbed by the leaves of submerged plants (Sutton & Bingham, 1968), but with emerged plants, the herbicide must be applied to the roots before it is translocated in the transpiration stream to the leaves (Sutton & Bingham, 1969).

Simazine can reduce the amount of dissolved oxygen in the aquatic environment twenty-four to forty-eight hours after treatment (Sutton, Evrard & Chappel, 1965 ; Sutton, Durham, Bingham & Foy, 1969). Removal of simazine from the water depends on absorption by the aquatic plants, adsorption to the soil, and dilution by running water. Of eight applications ranging from 2.0 to 4.0 p.p.m.w., approximately 65 per cent of the simazine was present in the water one week after the treatment (Sutton, Evrard & Bingham, 1966).

Another promising herbicide of the triazine family for control of emerged plants is 2-(ethylamino)-4-(isopropylamino)-6-(methylthio)-s-triazine (ametryne). Water hyacinth can be controlled with 4.5 kg ametryne/ha (Weldon & Blackburn, 1967). Low concentrations give considerable variation in control. Ametryne in combination with either 2,4–D or silvex has shown some promise for control of alligator weed. This chemical is absorbed by both the leaves and roots of plants and is translocated in either the xylem or phloem. Its toxic effect is principally as an inhibitor of photosynthesis.

Ureas. Several of the substituted urea herbicides are useful for control of certain aquatic plants. Apparently 3-(3,4-dichlorophenyl)-1,-1-dimethylurea (diuron) is the most effective, followed by 3-(p-chlorophenyl)-1,-1-dimethylurea (monuron) and 1-butyl-3-(3,4-dichlorophenyl)-1-methylurea (neburon) (Walker, 1965). The greatest potential of these herbicides appears to be as a pre-emergence or post-emergence treatment on emerged plants at approximately 30 kg/ha. Higher concentrations are required for algae and certain submerged plants. Fish and fish food organisms vary considerably in their susceptibility to these herbicides. Monuron has an EC_{50} value of 40 p.p.m.w. for bluegills. Neburon appears to be the most toxic of the substituted ureas mentioned.

In a simulated aquatic environment, appreciable loss of neburon and monuron did not occur until eight and sixteen weeks, respectively, after application of 45 kg/ha (Frank, 1966). A considerable amount of the herbicides penetrated the hydrosoil over a long period of time (128 days) and the rate of movement appeared to depend on the solubility of the chemicals.

Herbicide combinations. Combinations of herbicides have been used in aquatic weed control. Combinations of endothall and silvex, endothall and diquat, dalapon and TCA, and 2,4–D and silvex are a few sold for use in the United States of America. The combinations usually are manufactured to give the application a formulation with a broader spectrum of aquatic plant control.

Recently, laboratory and field screening studies with certain combinations of herbicides appeared to result in better control of some aquatic plants than when the herbicides were applied individually (Blackburn & Weldon, 1969 ; Mackenthum, Ingram & Porges, 1964). An increased phytotoxic effect was evident with the combination of diquat and CSP on some submerged plants. One of the causes related to this increased activity may be an increase of copper uptake by the plants in the presence of diquat (Sutton, Weldon & Blackburn, 1970). The authors also have research under way on the combination of copper with other herbicides. Preliminary data indicate that certain of these herbicides, when combined with copper containing compounds, may be as effective as diquat (Blackburn & Barlowe, 1970).

A new formulation technique. Controlled release of herbicides is one of the latest formulation techniques under study in the United States of America. Advantages of controlled release are reduced residue levels, increased herbicidal activity, lower toxicity to desired. fauna and flora, and reduced cost of weed control. Herbicides may be formulated as impregnated polyvinyl chloride, clay or casting plaster pellets ; or encapsulated in plastic polymers and impregnated rubber sheets.

Treatments with 2,4–D polyvinyl impregnated pellets on Eurasian watermilfoil (*Myriophyllum spicatum* L.) at 3 p.p.m.w. calculated on 100 per cent immediate release, gave excellent control within two weeks (Lawson, Barnes, Harris & Nelson, 1970). Water analysis indicated that 2,4-D did not exceed 0.4 p.p.m.w. throughout an eight-week test period. Similar results were obtained with endothall and dichlobenil.

In Florida, a clay pellet of the amine salt of endothall has given excellent control of submerged weeds in preliminary experiments. Herbicidal concentrations necessary for control have been reduced three to five fold depending on water flow. Similar results have been obtained with the encapsulated formulations of diquat, CSP, and endothall.

6.2.5   DISCUSSION

Control of aquatic weeds with herbicides is easier, faster and frequently less expensive than mechanical weed control. Improved herbicides used for controlling aquatic and bank weeds have low toxicity to humans and other warm-blooded animals. Several herbicides are harmless to fish and other aquatic organisms at concentrations necessary to control weeds. Many herbicides used in irrigated water will not injure crops at recommended rates. Nevertheless, the use of herbicides for aquatic weed control is being restricted. Public fears of side effects of herbicide in water resources threaten to reduce greatly the use of herbicides in water. The ambigous term 'potable water' and the multiple use of many water resources greatly complicate the use of herbicides for control of aquatic weeds. The conflict of interest in herbicidal control of aquatic weeds is well recognized in many areas of the world.

Adequate aquatic weed control will be necessary to assure continued use of water resources at present or future levels. To accomplish this, a benefit-hazard ratio must be established for each effective herbicide in each aquatic situation; and herbicides must continue to be used in the management programme, wherever the benefits will exceed the hazards by a reasonable margin. Application of herbicides in aquatic environments is an area of such sensitive public concern that the most careful attention must be given to observing all precautions and regulatory procedures.

Future research on herbicides should be directed toward persistence and fate in water, aquatic soil, fish, aquatic plants and crops irrigated with treated water. Additional information in these areas may reduce the public fear of using herbicides in water.

6.3. Biological control

F. D. Bennett,
Commonwealth Institute of Biological Control (CIBC), Curepe (Trinidad)

6.3.1 INTRODUCTION

Biological control is a relatively new and still largely untested method of controlling aquatic weeds. However, this method has worked very satisfactorily and at times quite spectacularly for selected terrestrial weeds, e.g. *Opuntia* spp. in Australia, South Africa and the West Indies, *Cordia curassavica* in Mauritius, etc., and initial investigations on a few of the more serious aquatic weeds indicate that it should be considered more widely particularly when introduced weeds are among the most important species.

The classical approach to biological control implies the introduction of a biotic agent into an area where an exotic pest occurs with the expectation that once this organism has been well established and widely disseminated it will provide perpetual control. More recently, increasing attention has been paid to the augmentation and encouragement of natural enemies already occurring in an area and the possibility of control of aquatic weeds by annual inoculative or inundative releases of either an exotic or a native organism is also receiving attention (Blackburn, Sutton & Taylor 1971).

While it has generally been accepted that introduced weeds are better candidates for biological control than native ones (the inference being that their natural enemies have not accompanied them), the possibilities that certain native weeds can be regulated by this method also exist. Each problem must necessarily be considered separately and the feasibility of this method evaluated.

The advantages of classical biological control, in comparison to other methods, are that it provides relatively low-cost, perpetual control with a minimum of detrimental side effects. On the other hand it is unlikely to be applicable to all aquatic weed problems. A considerable amount of time is required to carry out the research necessary to evaluate the effectiveness and host specificity of the control agents, and there is no guarantee that, in any particular instance, effective control will be achieved. However, it is generally agreed that the number of successes in a geographic area are related to the time and effort devoted to this method and that the benefits derived from successful examples more than offset the costs of projects where control has not occurred.

In general, the basic research, as well as the application of the biological method of control, is undertaken or sponsored by governmental or other large corporate bodies rather than by individuals. Although, as approved agents for specific weed problems become available, and methods for breeding and disseminating them are developed, it is probable that smaller institutions or individuals can supervise the biological control of specific aquatic weed problems in recreational lakes, hydro-electric reservoirs, home ponds, etc.

6.3.2 METHODS OF BIOLOGICAL CONTROL

In the classical approach to biological control of an introduced weed, investigations are undertaken of the biotic factors associated with the plant in its country of origin and/or similar factors associated with related species.

Agents which appear to have some potential are studied intensively and tested rigorously to ascertain that they do not attack economic crops or otherwise adversely effect the ecosystem. These, freed of their control agents (parasites, predators and pathogens) and with the approval of the appropriate government authorities, are introduced into the area where control is required. The procedures and criteria for selecting and testing insects and mites for the biological control of terrestrial weeds have been outlined by Zwölfer & Harris (1971). The traditional, classical approach to the biological control of terrestrial weeds has been to introduce organisms that are highly host specific with the aim of controlling a specific weed rather than a complex of unrelated species. However, there appears to be more latitude in the choice of agents for the biological control of aquatic weeds and less host specific organisms, which are tied by their biology to an aquatic environment, can be considered for introduction (Bennett, 1966, 1972).

To ensure that all undesirable disease organisms are excluded it may be necessary to breed the biotic agent for one or more generations under quarantine conditions in the country of origin, or the country where control is required, or at an intermediate point. It may then be necessary to undertake a mass breeding programme to ensure that adequate numbers are available for sequential releases in several areas. Provision should be made for a system of monitoring the progress of the biotic agents following their release to ascertain their rates of increase and dispersion and their effectiveness.

6.3.3 AGENTS FOR THE BIOLOGICAL CONTROL OF AQUATIC WEEDS

Whereas only insects, mites and disease organisms have been introduced for the control of terrestrial weeds, in addition snails, fishes and other vertebrates are under investigation for the control of aquatic weed problems (Bennett 1972 ; Blackburn, Sutton & Taylor 1971).

Insects and mites

For control of Alternanthera philoxeroides. The first and still most striking example of biological control of an aquatic weed by an insect is the introduction of the Chrysomelid beetle, *Agascicles hygrophila,* from Argentina into the United States, following exhaustive studies of its biology and host range, for the control of *Alternanthera philoxeroides.* This weed, introduced into the United States prior to 1900, had, by 1970, infested more than 27,000 hectares in the southern United States. The first releases were made in South Carolina in 1964, in Florida in 1965 and in California in 1964-65. Impressive control was reported initially at one release site near Jacksonville, Florida, and later at several other sites, although it either failed to establish or to provide an appreciable level of control at others. Studies have indicated that the effectiveness of *Agascicles hygrophila* is influenced by temperature, rate of water flow, plant habitat, nutrition, plant vigour and the interactions of these factors (Blackburn, Sutton & Taylor, 1971; Maddox, Andres, Hennessey, Blackburn & Spencer, 1971).

Two other insects, the thrips, *Amynothrips andersoni,* and the Phycitid moth, *Vogtia malloi,* were also cleared for trial against *A. philoxeroides* in the United States. While the performance of the thrips has not been impressive, *V. malloi,* cleared for release in 1970, has already caused impressive damage in Florida (N. R. Spencer, personal communication, May 1972). Whereas *A. hygrophila* can develop successfully only where the plant occurs as a true aquatic under conditions favouring vigorous plant growth, *V. malloi* is adapted to develop successfully on plants growing in semi-aquatic or terrestrial habitats and also under a wider range of climatic conditions.

For control of Salvinia spp. Although *Salvinia molesta (S. auriculata* auct.) was recorded as a pest of rice paddies in Sri Lanka prior to 1950 the possibilities of biological control were not investigated until the explosive growth form exhibited on the newly formed Kariba Lake appeared to threaten the future of the lake. Surveys of the natural enemies of *Salvinia* spp. were undertaken in Trinidad, and in northern South America in 1964, and three species of insects, the Acridid grasshopper *Paulinia acuminata,* the Curculionid weevil *Cyrtobagous singularis,* and the Pyralid moth *Samea multiplicalis Guenee,* were recommended for trial following studies on their host range in Brazil and Trinidad (Bennett, 1966). Releases of the grasshopper *P. acuminata* were made on both the Rhodesian and Zambian sides of Kariba Lake over the period 1969-71. The releases on the Zambian side were relatively small compared to liberations on the Rhodesian side of 2,000 nymphs and adults of the tropical Trinidad strain and 1,500 from subtropical Uruguay, but establishment has also occurred. Minor damage was evident during a survey in October 1971 (author's unpublished notes). By January 1972 population densities ranging from 1.6 to 9.4 adults per square metre were noted on the Rhodesian side and, by August, 20 to 30 per cent of the leaves were damaged where densities of three to four adults and nymphs per square metre were recorded (D. J. W. Rose, personal communication, 1972). Releases of the Trinidad strain on Lake Naivasha in 1970 were unsuccessful, although attempts have by no means been exhaustive. The daily drop in temperature occurring on the lake apparently militates against its increase. This species, as well as *C. singularis* and *S. multiplicalis,* is currently being released for the control of *S. molesta* on the Chobe River, Botswana, and, pending further study, may be released in India (CIBC correspondence).

For control of Eichhornia crassipes. The natural enemies of water hyacinth, *E. crassipes,* have been surveyed in South America (Coulson, 1971; Bennett & Zwölfer, 1968), in the West Indies and British Honduras (Bennett, 1970) and the United States (Bennett, 1970; Vogel & Oliver, 1969; Coulson, 1971). Seven species were recommended for further evaluation to determine whether they could be recommended for introduction into new areas. These are the stem-boring Crambine moth, *Acigona infusella* (Walk.) (= *A. ignitalis* Hmps.), the stem-boring Pyralid moth, *Epipagis albiguttalis* Hmps., the Acridid grasshoppers, *Cornops longicorne* and *C. aquaticum,* the Curculionid weevils, *Neochetina bruchi* and *N. eichhorniae,* which tunnel in the basal portions of the plant and the leaf-mining Galumnid mite *Orthogalumna terebrantis.* Host specificity tests undertaken in Argentina by USDA scientists and in Trinidad by CIBC have indicated that *N. eichhorniae* can be safely introduced and its release in the United States has been authorized (R. I. Sailer, personal communication, August 1972). It was released on the Kafue River, Zambia, in 1971 and below Lake McIlwaine in Rhodesia in 1972, the material originating

101

from Trinidad. *Epipagis albiguttalis* was sent from Trinidad to India where a disease-free culture was developed under quarantine and final host specificity tests were undertaken. Insects were then supplied to Zambia for release on the Kafue River, and to Rhodesia for release in areas where *E. crassipes* is a problem (CIBC unpublished documents). *O. terebrantis* has also been sent to India for rearing and transshipment to Zambia and Rhodesia. It has been recovered following releases in 1971 from the Kafue River. The North American Noctuid moth, *Arzama densa,* considered to be a potentially important control agent (Vogel & Oliver, 1969; Coulson, 1971) which warranted further study (Bennett, 1970) has subsequently been implicated as a pest of edible Araceae (D. Hadeck, personal communication, May 1972) and hence its introduction into other continents where this family is important should not be considered further.

The control of other aquatic weeds. Investigations on the insect fauna of several other aquatic weeds are in progress in various parts of the world. In India studies on a wide range of species financed by the United States Department of Agriculture have been in progress for several years (Sankaran, Srinath & Krishna, 1966 ; Sankaran, Menon, Narayanan, Krishna & Ranganath Bhat, 1970; Sankaran, Rao, Narayanan, Ramaseshiah, Krishaswamy & Krishna, 1971). These include *Myriophyllum intermedium, Nymphoides indica, Ludwigia adscendens, Potamogeton nodosus, Alternanthera* spp., *Nymphaea* spp. and *Pistia stratiotes,* and, for most species, one or more insects adapted to an aquatic environment have been found. Investigations at the Pakistan Station, CIBC, on the insects attacking *Hydrilla verticillata* have been initiated recently and nine species of insects have been encountered and are currently under study. These include three species of aquatic Curculionid weevils, *Bagous* spp., two species of *Hydrellia* flies (Diptera) mining the leaves and stems and three species of the aquatic moth, *Nymphula* (Baloch, Sanaullah & Ghani, 1971). The fauna attacking *Myriophyllum* spp. have also been studied in Pakistan where the weevils, *Bagous geniculatus, B. vicinus* and *Phylobus* sp., and the Gelechiid moth, *Aristotelia* sp., are considered to be adequately host specific to merit consideration for release in other countries (Baloch, Khan & Ghani, 1972). In Yugoslovia, *Myriophyllum spicatum* is attacked by several insects including the Pyraustid moth, *Paraponyx strationata,* and the Curculionid weevil, *Litodactylus leucogaster,* which are considered to be important biotic agents (Lekic, 1970; Lekic & Mihajlovic, 1970). Spencer (1971) has reared *Paraponyx* sp. from *M. spicatum* in Florida and has suggested that it may be a potential agent for use elsewhere.

Snails

Silva (1960) attempted to control a submerged aquatic weed reported under the name *Anacharis densa* by the use of the snail *Pomacea caniculata* in Brazil. Interest in North America stemmed from the discovery that a decline of *Australorbis glabratus,* the main intermediate snail vector for *Schistosoma mansoni,* followed the accidental introduction of the South American Marisa snail, *Marisa cornuarietis,* into Puerto Rico (Oliver-Gonzales, Baumer & Benson, 1956). Subsequent studies indicated that, in addition to its role as a predator of Planorbid snails, *M. cornuarietis* feeds avidly on a wide range of aquatic vegetation (Seaman & Porterfield, 1964). Investigations on *M. cornuarietis* in Puerto Rico (Ferguson & Butler, 1966) and more recent laboratory studies in Egypt (Demain & Lufty, 1964, 1965a, 1965b; Demain & Ibrahim, 1969) have been centred on its potential for reducing populations of Planorbid vectors of schistosomes and flukes, while other studies on its role as an agent for weed control have been carried out in Florida (Blackburn & Andres, 1968 ; Blackburn, Taylor & Sutton, 1971). Stocking rates (80,000 adults or 160,000 juveniles per hectare) necessary for the seasonal control of *Hydrilla (Hydrilla verticillata)* and southern naiad *(Naias guadelupensis)* Morong, have been worked out (Blackburn, Taylor & Sutton, 1971) and mass production techniques developed (Rich & Rouse, 1970). Annual stocking would be necessary where water temperatures drop below 10° C during winter (Blackburn, Taylor & Sutton, 1971).

There has been reluctance to recommend the introduction of this species into tropical areas outside the neotropics in the light of earlier experimental evidence that it damages seedling rice (Seaman & Porterfield, 1964) and its record as a pest of watercress in Trinidad. While further tests with seedling rice have somewhat allayed these fears (B. Hubendick, personal communication, 1972), a decision to release it in Egypt is still pending.

Blackburn, Sutton & Taylor (1971) have also briefly mentioned preliminary studies on *Pomacea australis* in which this species demonstrated a greater feeding capacity on submerged vegetation and a greater tolerance to low temperatures than *M. cornuarietis.* The same reservation stated for *M. cornuarietis,* i.e. a very wide host range, indicates that this species must be carefully evaluated before recommending its release.

Fish

Control by fish may occur in two ways, either by ingestion of plant tissue, or by stirring the hydrosoil, thus causing turbidity and thereby decreasing light so that the photosynthesis of rooted plants is adversely affected. While the role of fish in controlling aquatic weeds has long been recognized (Black, 1946 ; Schuster, 1952) attempts to manipulate species solely for the control of undesirable species have been made only comparatively recently. The early and also the current studies with fish are primarily concerned with their value as a source of human or animal food. The dual role of weed-control agents and protein source gives added initiative for investigating some of the more promising species and investigations with one or more species are currently under-way in many countries. There is, however, considerable concern over the possible detrimental effects on the various components of the ecosystem that may follow the introduction of exotic fish and thus use of this group of organisms, as well as the ones outlined previously, has to be considered carefully. The following species of fish are those currently receiving the most attention.

The grasscarp or white amur, *Ctenopharyngodon idella,* native to the large rivers of South China, has exhibited tolerance to a wide range of temperatures, to low oxygen levels, as well as to brackish water and Swingle (1957) considered it to be one of the most promising agents for biological control of rooted aquatics. It does not breed naturally outside China although spawning can be induced by the injection of fish pituary. Alabaster & Scott (1967) summarized the data of northern European workers on its food selectivity which indicated the favoured food plants to be Canadian pondweed, *Elodea canadensis,* hornwort *Ceratophyllum demersum* and duckweed *Lemna* spp., while the least favoured were rushes, *Juncus* spp. watercress *Rorippa (Nasturtium officinale),* and water-lily *Nuphar lutea.* Further evaluation of this species is in progress in England (Scott, Cross, Izard & Robson, 1971), in Central and Eastern Europe (Krupauer, 1971), in the United States (Blackburn & Sutton, 1971; Michenicz, Sutton & Blackburn, 1972*a,* 1972*b*) and elsewhere in the world (Hickling, 1965; Little, 1968). In its dual role as a source of food and weed-control agent *C. idella* is being stocked widely in Europe (Krupauer, 1971), Asia (Meta & Sharma, 1972) and Fiji (Hughes, 1972).

Since this species does not breed naturally outside China, rates of stocking of ponds, lakes, etc., could be calculated to permit the retention of an equitable amount of aquatic vegetation favourable to other desirable components of the ecosystem.

Blackburn, Sutton & Taylor (1971) have listed other species which have shown potential for control of certain aquatic plants. While the grasscarp appears to be one of the few species of interest for use in temperate climates, there are several others to be considered for trial in the subtropics and tropics. *Tilapia* spp. have been used most commonly, again in the dual role of a source of food and weed-control agents. The simultaneous stocking of the Congo by tilapia *T. rendalli* Boulanger (= *T. melanopleura* Dumeril) and *C. idella* to achieve control of a wider range of weeds has been recommended (Schuster, 1952).

Two South American species, *Metynnis roosevelti* and *Mylossoma argenteum*, both known as silver dollar, also merit trials as they attack several varieties of pondweeds (Yeo, 1967 ; Yeo & Fisher, 1970).

Other vertebrates

There are frequent references which indicate that domesticated animals—cows, pigs goats, ducks and geese—can play a useful role in controlling aquatic weeds (Little, 1968). However, these animals can be utilized only under special circumstances and are difficult to manage successfully for the control of weeds in large water impoundments or where purity of water is an important factor, although the possibilities of harvesting and processing aquatic weeds for livestock feed are being considered (Little, (ed.) 1968, 1968; see Chapter 7).

The manatee *Trichechus manatus* L. has received wide publicity as a potential biological agent (Allsopp, 1960 ; Sguros, Monkus & Phillips, 1965; Blackburn & Andres 1968), although Allsopp (1969) has pointed out some of the limitations and difficulties in attempting to utilize this species. While it is a voracious feeder it tends to graze selectively and, except in situations where it can be confined to a small area and thus forced to feed on all plants, it will bypass thick stands of one species to feed on another which it prefers. This factor, coupled with its scarcity, its low reproductive rate and the high cost of managing it, suggests that it is unlikely to be widely used in weed-control programmes.

The South American Coypu *Myocastor coypus* has also been suggested as a valuable agent for weed control as well as a useful fur-bearing animal. The relatively low value of its pelt, its omnivorous feeding habits and the damage to canal banks, dams, etc., caused by its burrowing activities suggest that it should not be recommended for introduction into areas where it does not occur.

Pathogens

The potential of pathogens such as viruses, fungi and bacteria still remains relatively unexplored. Wilson (1969) has reviewed the investigations which have been carried out. Parallel to the investigations on the insects attacking several aquatic weeds the Indian Station of the CIBC has over the past ten years studied the plant pathogens associated with them (Laudon & Ponnappa 1966 ; Ponnappa 1970; Nag Raj 1965, 1966 ; Nag Raj & Ponnappa 1969, 1970a, 1970b; Rao 1965, 1969). While it has been demonstrated that certain of the pathogens are not adequately host specific (Rao, 1969) to permit their use for weed control others, e.g. *Marasmiellus inoderma,* merit further investigations (Nag Raj, 1965). Recently full-time investigators have been recruited and a laboratory established at Gainesville, Florida, to study more fully the potential of certain of these pathogens as well as of others, as control agents of aquatic weeds (Zettler, Freeman, Rentz & Hill, 1971), and similar investigations are in progress at Boca Raton, Florida (Cappleman & Sturnock, 1972). In Nigeria an aphid-transmitted virus has been suggested as an important factor contributing to the annual dieback of *Pistia stratiotes* (Pettet & Pettet, 1970).

A viral disease of blue-green algae has been successfully used to control algae bloom in sewage disposal ponds (Jackson, 1967) and there is evidence that a complex of viruses associated with blue-green algae occurs (Safferman & Morris, 1967). As blue-green algae cause major problems in large reservoirs associated with major hydro-electric schemes, the possibilities of utilizing viruses for their control are being considered (see Wilson, 1969, for details).

The decline of Eurasian watermilfoil, *Myriophyllum spicatum,* along the upper Chesapeake Bay (United States) has been attributed to a disease possibly caused by a virus (Bayley & Southwick, 1968).

Many of the investigations with diseases are still in the experimental stage, but it appears probable that some of the weed problems, for which there may be no effective insect enemies, may be amenable to control by pathogens.

6.3.4   PLANT COMPETITION AND DISPLACEMENT

The possibilities of displacing or controlling aquatic weeds by the use of less noxious species have been attempted experimentally by Silva (1960) and discussed by Yeo & Fisher (1970). Certain of the submerged rooted species, e.g. *Myriophyllum* spp., may be more difficult to control with herbicides or mechanical removal than are floating species. The latter, if encouraged early in the season, may inhibit the growth or shade out submerged weeds. However, some of the floating species which provide the most complete surface coverage in the tropics are listed among the most serious weeds, e.g. *Eichhornia crassipes, Salvinia molesta* and *Pistia stratiotes,* and hence the consequences of utilizing this method particularly must be explored fully, if the use of an exotic competitor is contemplated.

6.3.5   DISCUSSION

The biological control of aquatic weeds is still in its infancy. Up to now, greatest success has been with insects, the group organisms most frequently utilized for the control of terrestrial weeds. For example successful control of *Alternanthera philoxeroides,* the first weed on which long-term, well-planned investigations were undertaken, has been achieved ; while investigations on *Salvinia* spp. and *Eichhornia crassipes* have suggested that an appreciable level of control, in some areas at least, may also be possible. However, it is probable that some of the most outstanding future successes of biological control of aquatic weeds will be with organisms other than insects and mites. It has been suggested that organisms with wider demonstrated host ranges than those used for terrestrial weed control can be introduced or manipulated for control of aquatic weeds but priority nevertheless should be given to host specific organisms when they occur. These are most likely to be insects, mites or pathogens, and hence those groups should be investigated in the early phases of biological control programmes, particularly in instances where an introduced weed is the major problem. Bennett (1972) has suggested that the important element of competition by other plant species is often lacking in situations where control of aquatic weeds is required and, therefore, the intensity of damage required to achieve control may have to be higher and more sustained than for the control of terrestrial weeds. On the other hand, it is possible that relatively minor injury by a primary organism may pave the way for the invasion of secondary organisms which cause the rapid collapse of the weed. As investigations involving several species of aquatic weeds in many parts of the world are in progress it is anticipated that much more definitive statements regarding the possibilities and application of biological control of these plants will be possible in the near future.

7. Utilization of aquatic plants

C. E. Boyd,
Fisheries Department, University of Auburn, Auburn,
Alabama (United States of America)

7.1 INTRODUCTION

Aquatic macrophytes have many actual or potential uses as compost, mulches, fertilizers, human food, feeds for livestock, sources of fibre for paper-making, and sources of various chemical substances (Sculthorpe, 1967; Little (ed.) 1968; Boyd, 1972). They can be woven into mats and baskets and are also used for the construction of dwellings and fences (Rudescu, Niculescu & Chivu, 1965), as well as for the purification of polluted effluents and water bodies (Boyd 1970c; Yount & Crossman, 1970; McNabb, Tiernay & Kosek, 1971; Seidel, 1971). Rice, *Oryza sativa*, is an emergent aquatic plant and the only vascular hydrophyte which is a major agronomic species. It is one of the world's main crops and forms the staple diet of over half the world's population. A small but important number of other aquatic crops exist, such as water chestnut *(Trapa spp.)*, lotus *(Nelumbo nucifera)* and watercress *(Nasturtium officinale)*. *Ipomoea aquatica* as one of the few aquatics grown as a green vegetable. Known as 'Ong Tsoi' in China and 'Kang Kong' in Malaysia, it is an important crop in Hong Kong where it supplies 15 per cent of the local vegetable output in a season (Edie & Ho, 1969). A number of aquatic plants are grown in small ponds for ornamental purposes and the sale of plants that are suitable for aquaria is of growing economic importance.

Utilization of natural communities of water weeds for human or animal food has received relatively little interest, but the extensive areas of water weeds in many tropical or warm temperate regions must be considered as a potential source of food which could be important to local populations. Shortages of food and large expanses of aquatic weeds often exist in the same locality and the utilization of these plants as food would convert a weed problem into a valuable crop. The use of aquatic plants as feed for livestock in technologically advanced nations will require the product to be competitive in quality and cost with conventional feeds. Pilot studies in the United States (Bailey, 1965) demonstrated that feeds of high quality can be made from several species of aquatic plants. However, the cost of harvesting and processing the plants by mechanical techniques prohibited commercial exploitation.

Aquatic plants may be useful in removing nutrients from waste waters. Schemes for cultivating aquatic plants in eutrophic waters to remove nutrients and control the growth of phytoplankton have promise (Yount & Crossman, 1970). Nutrients can be removed from eutrophic lakes by harvesting natural communities of aquatic plants (Boyd, 1970c, 1971a). Plants removed in pollution abatement programmes can be used as feeds for livestock or as green manures.

Sculthorpe (1967) has presented an excellent review of the past and present utilization of aquatic plants for horticultural, medicinal and miscellaneous other commercial uses. Little (ed.) (1968) compiled a most useful handbook on the utilization of aquatic plants with special reference to *Eichhornia crassipes* and other weed species. Extracts from a large number of publications from different parts of the world are given and these provide an essential reference to anyone investigating the possible utilization of a particular aquatic weed. Sharma (1971) has reviewed the eradication and utilization of *Eichhornia crassipes* particularly in Asia. Finally, Boyd (1972) has recently compiled a bibliography of articles dealing with this subject. In this chapter, only a brief review of selected aspects of the utilization of aquatic plants will be possible and the works referred to above should be consulted for the full range of possibilities that exist.

7.2   AQUATIC PLANTS AS FOOD FOR LIVESTOCK

7.2.1   *Chemical composition*

In addition to being palatable and non-toxic, a good feed for livestock must contain adequate levels of protein, fat, carbohydrate, vitamins and mineral nutrients for satisfactory growth. The feed should have a fairly low fibre content so that most of the organic matter is highly digestible even to non-ruminant animals. Dried alfalfa (lucerne) hay prepared from succulent plants harvested prior to flowering had the following proximate composition ; crude protein (nitrogen x 6.25) 18.6 per cent, fat 2.6 per cent, fibre 23.7 per cent, and ash (mineral matter) 8.6 per cent (Morrison, 1961). Dried samples of several other conventional forages have a similar proximate composition so alfalfa hay is a suitable standard for comparison with aquatic plants.

Boyd (1968, 1969*b*) and Straskraba (1968) have determined the proximate composition of a variety of species of aquatic plants which were harvested while still in a young, lush stage of growth. There was considerable interspecific variation in concentrations of crude protein, ash, fibre and fat. The proximate composition of dried samples of many species showed that they were inferior to alfalfa hay for use as livestock feed, but several species were as suitable, or better, than dried alfalfa. On the average, aquatic plants contained less crude protein, somewhat more ash and fat, and slightly less fibre than alfalfa hay. Submerged and floating plants usually had higher values for crude protein and ash than emergent and floating-leaved plants. Average values for the proximate composition of some water weeds which appear suitable as feeds are presented in Table 11.

Amino acid concentrations were determined for fourteen species of water weeds (Boyd, 1969*b*, 1970*e*). Although there were large differences in total concentrations of protein in different species, the percentage of the total protein constituted by each amino acid was fairly constant for all species and did not differ greatly from those reported for forage crops by Altschul (1958). Crude protein usually overestimated true protein (sum of all amino acids) in aquatic plants by only 10 to 20 per cent and, therefore, is a suitable estimate of protein content for general purposes. The digestibility of protein in plant materials decreases with increasing concentrations of tannins. Concentrations of tannins of 10 per cent or more of the dry weight were found in *Myriophyllum brasiliense, Cabomba caroliniana, Ludwigia peruviana, L. stolonifera, Brasenia schreberi,* and *Nymphaea odorata* (Boyd, 1968). The digestibility of the protein in these species would be greatly impaired.

Concentrations of inorganic elements in most species of aquatic plants fall within the range of values reported for crop plants and deserve no special mention (Boyd, 1969*b;* Reimer & Toth, 1968, 1969, 1970). Submerged aquatic plants from hard-water often have marl encrustations on external surfaces which greatly increase the

Table 11. Proximate composition (percentage dry weight) of some aquatic plants (each value is the average of three to fifteen samples; all samples represent plants which were in a lush, green stage of growth)

Species	Ash	Crude protein[1]	Fat[2]	Cellulose[3]
Eichhornia crassipes[4]	18.0	17.1	3.6	28.2
Pistia stratiotes[4]	21.1	13.1	3.7	26.1
Nelumbo lutea[5]	10.4	13.7	5.2	23.6
Nuphar advena[5]	6.5	20.6	6.2	23.9
Nymphoides aquatica[6]	7.6	9.3	3.3	37.4
Potamogeton diversifolius[6]	22.7	17.3	2.8	30.9
Najas guadalupensis[6]	18.7	22.8	3.8	35.6
Ceratophyllum demersum[6]	20.6	21.7	6.0	27.9
Hydrilla verticillata[6]	27.1	18.0	3.5	32.1
Egeria densa[6]	22.1	20.5	3.3	29.2
Typha latifolia[7]	6.9	10.3	3.9	33.2
Justicia americana[7]	17.4	22.9	3.4	25.9
Sagittaria latifolia[7]	10.3	17.1	6.7	27.6
Alternanthera philoxeroides[7]	13.9	15.6	2.7	21.3
Orontium aquaticum[7]	14.1	19.8	7.8	23.9

1. Nitrogen x 6.25.
2. Ether-extractable material.
3. Cellulose values are slightly lower than values for crude fibre.
4. Floating species.
5. Floating-leaved species.
6. Submerged species.
7. Emergent species.

proportion of inorganic to organic matter. Ash values of 25 to 50 per cent of the dry weight are not uncommon in such plants. Feeds prepared from marl-encrusted plants would be of low nutritive value, but would be useful as a calcium supplement in diets of low calcium content.

There are considerable variations in the concentrations of most chemical constituents in samples of an aquatic plant species and this makes it difficult to predict the usefulness of a particular stand of plants. Concentrations may vary two fold or more when plants harvested at similar stages of maturity, but from different sites, are compared. For example, crude protein values for *Typha latifolia* shoots from twenty-nine sites ranged from 5.4 to 13.2 per cent of the dry weight. Concentrations of various constituents also increase or decrease as plants mature. For example, the crude protein content of dried shoots of *Justicia americana* from the same population decreased from 22.8 per cent on 19 May to 12.7 per cent on 1 September.

7.2.2 Standing crops of aquatic plants

For a species of wild vegetation to be useful as a feed, it must obviously be of good nutritive quality. Furthermore, extensive stands containing sufficient amounts of material to justify harvest must be present. The stands should be fairly monospecific, or at least contain assemblages of species with similar nutritive values, so that the quality of the harvested product is predictable. Many aquatic weeds fulfil these conditions. Extensive, almost pure stands of emergent species are common in shallow-water habitats of most climatic regions. Floating species such as *Salvinia molesta (S. auriculata* auct.), *Eichhornia crassipes,* and *Pistia stratiotes,* may cover hundreds or even thousands of hectares in tropical regions (Holm, Weldon & Blackburn, 1969; Mitchell, 1969; see Chapter 3). Submerged and floating-leaved vegetation often occurs in communities which contain several species, but many submerged plants have high concentrations of nutrients and feeds prepared from most assemblages of species would have fair to good proximate compositions.

As one would expect, different species differ greatly on their inherent ability to produce dry matter. Large standing crops of dry matter are found in tall, emergent plants and values of ten to twenty tons of shoots/ha are sometimes found in species such as *Typha latifolia, Schoenplectus (scirpus) validus, Saururus cernuus, Panicum hemitonium* and *Juncus effusus.* However, depending on the stage of growth of the plants, emergent species which produce large standing crops of dry matter usually have a higher fibre content and a lower protein content than emergent species which produce lower standing crops of dry matter. Thus, species such as *Justicia americana, Alternanthera philoxeroides* and *Pontederia cordata* are of higher quality as feeds, though they normally have shoot standing crops of 4 to 8 t/ha. Large floating plants may also have large standing crops and values of dry matter above 10 t/ha are commonly encountered in *Eichhornia crassipes,* other floating plants usually having standing crops below 5 t/ha. Floating plants are harvested intact and, even though roots have a less favourable proximate composition than shoots, dried samples of intact plants usually have adequate concentrations of nutrients. Submerged and floating-leaved plants normally have standing crops of shoots which range from 1 to 5 t/ha.

The suitability of the site for growth also influences the standing crop of a particular species. For example, standing crops of shoots in *Typha latifolia* at twenty-nine sites ranged from 4.3 to 22.5 t/ha and production of shoots by *Typha latifolia* was found to increase with increasing quantities of available phosphorus. However, contrary to general belief, pollution of bodies of water with plant nutrients does not necessarily increase production of water weeds. Frequently, excessive concentrations of dissolved nutrients may stimulate dense growths of phytoplankton which prevent light from penetrating to the bottom soils and eliminate many higher plants. Dense growths of submerged species are never found in eutrophic waters which produce high densities of phytoplankton.

Standing crops of selected aquatic plants are summarized in Table 12. All these species are capable of producing stands which are dense enough to justify harvest provided a sufficient area is colonized as shown by comparison with yields of dry matter for forage crops. Morrison (1961) gave average yields of alfalfa hay and corn silage in the United States as 4.5 and 5.0 t/ha, respectively, though these two crops will commonly produce 8 to 10 t/ha under proper management. It is remarkable that unmanaged stands of some water plants produce as much or more dry matter per unit area as is produced by crop species which were selected for high yield and cultured under near-optimum conditions.

Table 12. Typical standing crop values for some common aquatic plants

Species	dry weight (t/ha)	Source
Eichhornia crassipes[1]	12.8	Penfound (1956)
Pistia stratiotes[1]	4.6	Odum (1957)
Azolla pinnata[1]	2.8	Gopal (1967)
Ceratophyllum demersum[2]	6.8	Forsberg (1960)
Myriophyllum verticillatum[2]	2.4	Forsberg (1960)
Potamogeton pectinatus[2]	2.2	Low & Bellrose (1944)
Najas guadalupensis[2]	1.1	Low & Bellrose (1944)
Nymphoides aquatica[3]	1.8	Boyd (1968)
Nelumbo lutea[2]	1.0	Boyd (1968)
Nuphar advena[3]	0.8	Polisini & Boyd (1972)
Typha latifolia[4]	15.3	Penfound (1956)
T. domingensis[4]	14.8	Polisini & Boyd (1972)
Alternanthera philoxeroides[4]	7.4	Boyd (1968)
Sagittaria latifolia[4]	7.3	Boyd (1968)
Eleocharis quadrangulata[4]	7.2	Polisini & Boyd (1972)
Pontederia cordata[4]	7.2	Polisini & Boyd (1972)
Justicia americana[4]	7.1	Boyd (1968)
Orontium aquaticum[4]	2.4	Polisini & Boyd (1972)

1. Floating species.
2. Floating-leaved species.
3. Submerged species.
4. Emergent species.

7.2.3 Harvesting and drying

The most obvious use of water weeds is to harvest the shoots or whole plants and feed them to livestock and various methods of mechanical removal of these plants are discussed in Chapter 6. Large floating plants such as *Eichhornia crassipes* and *Pistia stratiotes* can be lifted from the water by hand or with a hay fork. Smaller floating plants such as *Lemna* or *Azolla* can best be removed with small mesh seines or dip nets. Submerged plants can be harvested by pulling rakes through the under-water meadows. Emergent and floating-leaved plants can be cut at the desired height with knives, or in areas with loose bottom soil, pulled from the substrate by hand. One man can harvest 1,500 kg or more of fresh weight of plants per day from moderately dense stands of most species. Various mechanical devices mounted on boats or barges have been developed for large-scale harvesting and are discussed in Chapter 6.

The period of harvesting is important as the concentrations of crude protein in many species decline as the plants age and, generally, plants should be harvested while they are still in a young, succulent stage of growth. For example, the standing crops of shoots in a *Justicia americana* population were 5.0 kg/ha on 19 May, 5.6 kg/ha on 5 June, 7.0 kg/ha on 1 July, and 7.1 kg/ha on 3 August. The harvestable crude protein values for these dates were 1.1, 1.2, 1.3 and 1.2 kg/ha, respectively. There was as much crude protein present on 19 May as on any subsequent date and less material had to be handled to obtain it. Furthermore, plants from the earlier harvest are more digestible and some species will regrow, allowing more than one harvest per year.

Many water weeds, especially floating and submerged species, have a high water content (90 to 95 per cent) and must be at least partially dehydrated. This can be accomplished by placing the plants in thin layers on a sloping wooden, concrete or metal surface ; or draping them over suspended rope or wire, allowing the adherent water to drain away, and leaving them to dry in the sun until the desired degree of dehydration is obtained. It is important to turn the plants at intervals to decrease decay. Species with a lower moisture content of 80 to 85 per cent can be used as a feed without dehydration, but other species must be dried to increase the food value per unit weight. The importance of this is illustrated by comparing the crude protein content of fresh and dried aquatic plants to that of fresh and dry alfalfa (Fig. 16). Aquatic plants compare favorably on a dry weight basis, but not on a fresh weight basis. Mechanical methods of drying vegetation are expensive and of questionable practicality for use in the preparation of feeds from aquatic plants.

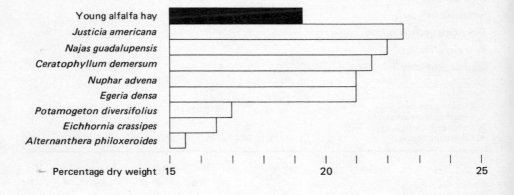

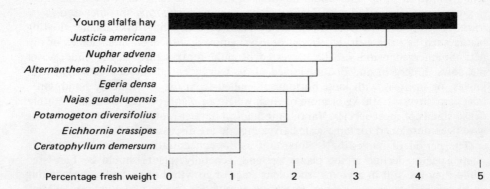

Figure 16. A comparison of the percentage crude protein of young alfalfa hay with the crude protein content of eight aquatic plants. The comparison is made on a dry weight and a fresh weight basis.

7.3 LEAF PROTEIN FROM AQUATIC PLANTS

Preparation of leaf protein involves the extraction of protein from freshly harvested leaves or shoots by crushing the plants, pressing the juice from the pulp and coagulating the protein in the juice by heating. The curd of protein is filtered out and dried. Leaf protein is suitable for use in human diets. Pirie (1971) discusses techniques for extracting and separating leaf protein. The high water content of aquatic plants facilitates the extraction of their protein. Boyd (1968) evaluated the extractibility of proteins from twenty-five species of water weeds. The yields of protein from most species were low. A few species appeared suitable as raw material for protein extraction and the following quantities of protein were obtained in leaf protein isolates: *Justicia americana* 590 kg/ha, *Alternanthera philoxeroides* 478 kg/ha, *Sagittaria latifolia* 362 kg/ha, *Nymphaea odorata* 197 kg/ha and *Polygonum sp.* 180 kg/ha. Leaf protein from aquatic plants was similar in chemical composition to leaf protein from crop plants. Research should be extended to include other species. Additional information on leaf protein from aquatic plants has been presented by Boyd (1971*b*).

7.4 UTILIZATION OF REED SWAMPS

Extensive stands of aquatic plants, particularly emergents in marsh systems, have been utilized for a wide variety of purposes ranging from the construction of houses and boats to pulping for paper. *Cyperus papyrus* was used by the ancient Egyptians for making papyrus and the recent voyage of a papyrus boat across the Atlantic demonstrates the suitability of this type of material for boat construction. More recently, *Phragmites* has been harvested mechanically in Poland and Denmark and used for housing and fencing material. However the most spectacular example of the successful utilization of this type of aquatic plant is the development of mechanized harvesting and processing techniques in the reed swamps of the Danube delta, Romania (Rudescu *et al.*, 1965). The plants in the area had been used locally for housing and fencing material for a long time, but, since 1956, they have also been exploited industrially. As techniques improved, the quantities of plants harvested increased from some tens of thousands of tons harvested per year between 1956 and 1958, to 200,000 tons at the present. Development of the utilization of these reed swamps has been based on manipulation of the hydrological régime, efficient methods of harvesting and storing *Phragmites* and the industrial processing of the material for cellulose fibre, as well as for a number of other side products, including furfurol, alcohol, yeast and fertilizers.

7.5 COMPOSTS, MULCHES AND FERTILIZERS

Several aquatic weeds have been used to make composts, mulches and fertilizers and a variety of methods are given in Little (ed.) (1968). For example Watson (1947) describes how compost can be made from *Eichhornia crassipes* in India. The plant is first allowed to dry until it wilts. It is then mixed with wood ash, earth and manure, and placed in special bamboo frames. The process of fermentation, thus initiated, causes the temperature to rise to 60° C. If successful, the material will break down

113

within about three weeks to a month and can be used after a further two months. Singh (1962) compared the use of compost made from a number of aquatic weeds such as *Pistia, Hydrilla, Najas, Ottelia* and *Eichhornia.*

Salvinia molesta has been used as a mulch on gardens in the vicinity of Lake Kariba. It is particularly useful if mixed with the dung from game animals such as elephant and buffalo or when placed in a chicken run for some days beforehand, so that it partially dries out and becomes mixed with the chicken droppings.

7.6 REMOVAL OF NUTRIENTS AND OTHER CHEMICALS

Aquatic plants can possibly be employed to remove nutrients from waste-water effluents prior to their release into natural or impounded waters. Effluents could be passed through holding ponds containing populations of aquatic plants which would absorb nutrients and reduce their concentrations in the effluents. Plants for use in these systems must be capable of absorbing large quantities of nitrogen and phosphorus, the two nutrients most frequently associated with eutrophication, and have rapid growth rates. *Eichhornia crassipes* appears to be an ideal plant for removing nutrients. As long as space is available for growth and weather conditions are favourable, new plants are rapidly produced by vegetative means. By continually removing a portion of the population, it is possible to maintain a proportion of rapidly growing plants within the population. This insures that at least a portion of the population is growing and absorbing nutrients at all times. Pilot studies indicate that up to 29 t/ha of dry weight of *Eichhornia* can be produced in ponds receiving additions of nutrients (Wahlquist, 1972). This harvest of plants would include 157 kg/ha of phosphorus and 693 kg/ha of nitrogen.

Certain species of aquatic plants could be cultivated in specified areas of excessively eutrophic waters to remove nutrients and thereby reduce densities of phytoplankton. An excellent example of the utility of this scheme is afforded by research on fish culture. Large quantities of fish feeds are applied to ponds containing intensive cultures of channel catfish *(Ictalurus punctatus).* Waste feed and excretory products from the fish supply adequate nitrogen and phosphorus for development of dense blooms of phytoplankton which cause shallow thermal and chemical stratification. Large quantities of dead plankton and waste products from the fish culture accumulate in the hypolimnion. Upwelling of oxygen deficient waters caused by winds or cold rains may result in oxygen depletion and fish kills. Blooms of phytoplankton may also die suddenly and their subsequent decay cause oxygen depletion and fish kills. *Eichhornia crassipes* plants were contained in barriers and allowed to cover 10 per cent of the surface of ponds. These plants removed enough nutrients to reduce the density of phytoplankton and decrease the probability of fish kills. Older plants are continuously removed from the pond to prevent the return of nutrients to the system when they die.

Plant nutrient levels in some shallow, weed-infested, eutrophic lakes could be reduced by removal of native vegetation. However, lakes with large areas of shallow water where light penetrates to the bottom are ideal habitats for submerged plants and some species will regrow following harvest. Even when sufficient nutrients were removed from a shallow lake for it to revert to an oligotrophic system, submerged plants would still be the dominant vegetation.

Recently, Seidel (1971) described experiments with a variety of aquatic plants and showed that these were capable of absorbing inorganic ions and metabolizing complex organic substances, such as phenols, contained in waste waters. Furthermore, it appears that some aquatic plants such as *Scirpus lacustris* produced exudates which had a toxic effect against bacteria, such as *Escherichia coli,* and the possibility of using them to purify sewage from hospitals is being investigated.

8. An appraisal of the problem of aquatic weeds

D. S. Mitchell
(United Kingdom)

Human progress depends in part upon man's ability to regulate and control water supplies to suit his requirements. As he has acquired and developed the technological skill to manage resources by controlling floods, conserving water in reservoirs, tapping its underground resources, pumping or piping it from wet to arid regions, or using it as a medium for transport, so have the problems caused by aquatic plants increased. Unfortunately man's skill at, and knowledge of, engineering have not been matched by his understanding of the intricacies of biological systems and his ability to maintain them in a stable condition. Man's history shows him, for the most part, to be a despoiler of ecosystems and, from bitter experience, he has learnt that there is a limit to nature's bounty. Nevertheless, human endeavours in agriculture have met with marked success in many cases. Most of these have involved the management of simplified systems with a severely reduced diversity of species. However, while it has been possible to reduce certain terrestrial systems to virtual monocultures, it has proved to be considerably more difficult to do this with aquatic systems, largely because the mobility of the water medium results in the dilution and transference of man's attempts at regulating the system. Thus, only small bodies of water, such as ponds, are normally amenable to the closely controlled type of management represented by many agricultural systems. Large bodies of water are more difficult and the management of these with their complex of many species is more closely analogous with the management of game parks and similar natural terrestrial systems, where the record also shows evidence of failure more often than of success in maintaining ecological stability.

The problems caused by aquatic vegetation must be seen in this context. As indicated in the first chapter, aquatic plants are weeds only in so far as they interfere with man's utilization of, or purpose for, a body or water. But it has also been shown that man himself is frequently an important agent in creating the conditions which promote the occurrence of excessive growths of aquatic vegetation. It is logical, therefore, that courses of action which give rise to such difficulties should be avoided or, at least, used with due consideration for the possible outcome. It is the unexpectedness and surprising severity of many aquatic weed problems that often seem to magnify the problem to apparently uncontrollable levels. Thus it is possible that the impact of problems may be lessened if they had been predicted and methods of handling them were already available. In the past, research on aquatic weeds has been concentrated on means of countering existing weed problems and their effects, principally by technological means. There has been far too little work on the factors which led up to a problem and, in many cases, these have not even been identified, let alone their mode of action investigated. In the same way, not enough is known about the plants themselves and their reaction to various environmental factors, and even less about the structure, function and behaviour of the whole ecosystem, of which they form a part.

Man's objective must be to improve his ability to counteract the adverse effects of aquatic vegetation by controlling the extent of existing problem populations of aquatic weeds, and by preventing, or limiting, the seriousness of future occurrences. In order to fulfil this objective future research should be aimed at improving man's ability :

1. To predict the occurrence of aquatic weed problems, as well as the outcome of management policies.
2. To deal with existing problems by designing effective management procedures which have no unacceptable, detrimental side effects.

The ability of the hydrobiologist to predict the behaviour and response of aquatic ecosystems as a whole, or in part, is dependent on his knowledge of the structure and mode of function of the system under a range of different conditions. Basic research, which will give him that knowledge, is urgent and essential. It is urgent because it is, by nature, long-term research which will not provide immediate answers. Thus it is necessary that this type of research should be continuously encouraged and not just when problems occur. This type of basic research is essential because, without it, mankind will continue to despoil his environment without being aware of what he is doing and will have to continue his attempts at environmental management largely by trial and error, rather than by rationally designed management programmes. The use of computer modelling has been advocated as a powerful tool in improving man's powers of prediction in this field. Improved prediction should lead to greater preparedness so that means would be available to deal with aquatic weeds at an early stage in the development of excessively large populations.

Procedures for handling aquatic weed problems typically fall into four phases: identification; control selection; control implementation; and management. The identification phase is concerned with the decision that a population of plants is causing a problem requiring control, and with the specific identification of the plant or plants in question. The factors that should be considered in the classification of a plant as a weed were outlined in the first chapter. The determination of the specific name of the plant, if it is a well-known weed, is facilitated by the availability of appropriate illustrated publications. The production of Cook's manual, which is now in preparation, will be of immense value in improving this aspect of aquatic weed problems. However, regional texts such as those produced by Wild (1961), Weldon, Blackburn & Harrison (1969) and Bristow, Cardenas, Fullerton & Sierra (1972) have been most useful and should be more widely used to educate people concerned with water resources about the identity and appearance of potentially dangerous species.

The second phase of an aquatic weed problem involves the selection of the most appropriate methods for dealing with the problem on the basis of the financial costs and benefits involved. It is desirable that a number of alternative methods are examined (see Mulligan, 1969, for example). These should be evaluated separately and in combination. In each case, there should be an assessment of the ecological impact of the measures and a benefit/cost analysis of their implementation. It is important that one of the alternatives that is analysed and assessed is that of taking no action against the weed. As stated earlier, most of the research, that has been carried out so far with aquatic weeds, has been concerned with control and this subject has been reviewed in Chapter 6. However, it is now realized that selection of the most appropriate method depends not only on the effectiveness of the agent against the weed, but also on its effect on the ecosystem as a whole. For instance, herbicides, such as sodium arsenite, which are toxic to a wide spectrum of plant and animal species, should be avoided in favour of those with a more specific action. The effects of weed control treatments on the whole ecosystem are currently under active investigation in many research centres and there is no doubt that the knowledge being gained will improve the management of weed problems. It is also likely that procedures will become increasingly more complex and possibly involve the integration of different control methods, the application of which would depend on the seasonal growth of the weed, and the response of the environment to the treatment. It is clear that research into different methods of control must be actively continued in order that a large number of alternative methods of containing aquatic weed problems should be available for selection.

The third phase, in which the selected methods are implemented, is one with considerable implications to the formulation of long-term management procedures. It is important to establish, at the outset, a programme of regular assessment of the effect of the control measures on the weed, and on the ecosystem as a whole. The proper design of such a programme also demands a basic knowledge of the structure and function of the system and, in many cases, this is inadequate at present. However, for the moment, monitoring programmes could be formulated on the basis of previous experience with disturbed ecosystems.

While it is clear that further research is required on a number of aspects of the first three phases of an aquatic weed problem, the greatest room for improvement is in the administrative procedures by which aquatic weed problems are handled. Too often, there are expensive delays between the realization that there is an aquatic weed problem and the selection of appropriate control measures, and between the selection of the measures and their implementation. It is obvious that these delays can cause a possibly manageable weed population to become virtually unmanageable.

The fourth phase is a long-term one in which a management policy is formulated on the basis of the experience of implementing control measures in the third phase. The management programme may include preventive as well as ameliorative measures and must not conflict with the pattern of utilization for the water body. Consideration should also be given to the economical and ecological implications of the programme. Present knowledge of aquatic ecosystems is inadequate, in most cases, to formulate ecologically sound programmes of management. Thus, it is important that the systems to which these are applied are regularly checked for undesirable changes. The monitoring procedures required for this are a continuation of those initiated in phase three and must form an important part of the programme. This situation also demands that alternative management procedures are readily available to be introduced if necessary.

In most cases the means to control undesirable aquatic vegetation by either chemical or mechanical methods are available, provided the cost can be met. Knowledge of the biological interactions involved, including those that are operative in biological control measures, is not available to the same extent and it is here that future research effort must be concentrated if mankind is to become the benevolent manipulator of his environment he ought to be, rather than the destructive despoiler he so often is at present.

References

Alabaster, J. S.; Stott, B. 1967. Grasscarp (*Ctenopharyngodon idella* Val.) for aquatic weed control. *Proc. Eur. Weed Res. Coun. 2nd Int. Symp. Aquat. Weeds 1967*, p. 123-6.

Allsopp, W. H. L. 1960. The manatee: ecology and use for weed control. *Nature, (Lond.)*, no. 188, p. 762.

—. 1969. Aquatic weeds control by manatees—its prospects and problems. *Man-made lakes. The Accra symposium*, p. 344-51. Edited by L. E. Obeng. Accra, Ghana Universities Press.

Altschul, A. M. (ed.). 1958. *Processed plant protein foodstuffs*. New York, Academic Press.

American Fisheries Society. 1967. *Reserv. Fish. Resour. Symp. April 5-7, 1967, Athens, Georgia.* Washington, D.C., Am. Fish. Soc.

American Geophysical Union. In press. *Int. Symp. Man-made Lakes, Knoxville, Tenn.* Washington, D.C.

American Public Health Association. 1971. *Standard methods for the examination of water and wastewater.* 13th ed. New York.

Anon. 1962. *Drinking water standards.* U.S. Dept. of Health, Educ. and Welfare. 36 p. Public Health Service pub. no. 956.

Arber, A. 1920. *Water plants—a study of aquatic angiosperms.* Cambridge, Cambridge University Press.

Arle, H. F. 1950. The effect of aromatic solvents and other aquatic herbicides on crop plants and animals. *Proc. West. Weed Contr. Conf.*, vol. 12, p. 58-60.

Armstrong, J. F. 1872. On the naturalised plants of the Province of Canterbury. *Trans. N.Z. Inst.*, Vol. 4, p. 284-90. Cited by Chapman (1970).

Bailey, T. A. 1965. Commercial possibilities of dehydrated aquatic plants. *Proc. Sth. Weed Contr. Conf.*, Vol. 18, p. 543-51.

Baloch, G. M.; Sanaullah; Ghani, M. A. 1971. Insects and other organisms attacking *Hydrilla verticillata. Commonw. Inst. Biol. Contr. a. Rep. 1971.*

Baloch, G. M.; Khan, A. G.; Ghani, M. A. 1972. Phenology, biology, and host-specificity of some stenophagous insects attacking *Myriophyllum* spp. in Pakistan. *Hyacinth Contr. J.*, vol. 10, p. 13-16.

Barrett, P. R. F.; Robson, T. O. 1971. The effect of time of application on the susceptibility of some emergent water plants to dalapon. *Proc. Eur. Weed Res. Coun. 3rd Int. Symp. Aquat. Weeds 1971*, p. 197-203.

Bayley, S. R. H.; Southwick, C. H. 1968. Recent decline in the distribution and abundance of Eurasian milfoil in Chesapeake Bay. *Chesapeake Sci.*, vol. 9, p. 177-81.

Beadle, L.; Lind, E. 1960. Research on the swamps of Uganda. *Uganda J.*, vol. 24, p. 84-7.

Beauchamp, R. S. A. 1953. Sulphates in African inland waters. *Nature* (Lond.), no. 171, p. 769-71.

Bennett, F. D. 1966. Investigations on the insects attacking the aquatic ferns *Salvinia* spp. in Trinidad and northern South America. *Proc. Sth. Weed Contr. Conf.*, vol. 19, p. 497-504.

—. 1970. Insects attacking water hyacinth in the West Indies, British Honduras and the USA. *Hyacinth Contr. J.*, vol. 8, p. 10-13.

—. 1972. Some aspects of the biological control of aquatic weeds. *Proc. 2nd Int. Symp. Biol. Contr. Weeds, Rome, 1971.*

Bennett, F. D.; Zwölfer, H. 1968. Exploration for natural enemies of the water hyacinth in northern South America and Trinidad. *Hyacinth Contr. J.*, vol. 7, p. 44-52.

Bennett, G. W. 1962. *Management of artificial lakes and ponds.* New York, Reinhold Publ. Corp., 291 p.

Betson, R. P.; Eklund, C. D.; Joyce, R. T.; Kilmer, V. J.; Lutz, J. F.; Mason, D. D.; Mc Cracken, R. J.; Nelson, L. A.; Woodhouse, W. W. 1970. *Watershed research in western North Carolina.* Knoxville, Tenn., Tennessee Valley Authority.

119

Biggar, J. W.; Corey, R. B. 1969. Agricultural drainage and eutrophication. *Eutrophication: causes, consequences, correctives,* p. 404-45. Washington, D.C., National Academy of Sciences.

Bill, S. M. 1969. The water weed problem in Australia. *Hyacinth Contr. J.,* vol. 8, p. 1-6.

Billings, W. D. 1964. *Plants and the ecosystem.* London, Macmillan.

Black, J. D. 1946. Nature's own weed killing the German carp. *Wisc. Conserv. Bull.,* vol. 11, p. 3-7.

Blackburn, Robert D. 1966. Weed control in fish ponds in the United States. *Proc. Wld.Symp. Warm-water Pond Fish,* vol. 5, p. 1-17. (FAO fish. rept., no. 44).

Blackburn, R. D.; Andres, L. A. 1968. The snail, the mermaid, and the flea beetle. *Yb. U.S. Dep. Agric.,* p. 229-34.

Blackburn, R. D.; Barlowe, W. C. 1970. Copper combinations on submerged aquatic weeds. *Proc. So. Weed Conf.,* vol. 23, p. 311.

Blackburn, R. D.; Sutton, D. L. 1971. Growth of the white amur *(Ctenopharyngodon idella* Val.) on selected species of aquatic plants. *Proc. Eur. Weed Res. Coun. 3rd Int. Symp. Aquat. Weeds 1971,* p. 87-93.

Blackburn, R. D.; Sutton, D. L.; Taylor, T. M. 1971. Biological control of aquatic weeds. *J. Irrig. Drain. Div. Am. Soc. Civ. Engrs.,* vol. 97, p. 421-32.

Blackburn, R. D.; Taylor, T. M.; Sutton, D. L. 1971. Temperature tolerance and necessary stocking rates of *Marisa cornuarietis* L. for aquatic weed control. *Proc. Eur. Weed Res. Coun. 3rd Int. Symp. Aquat. Weeds 1971.* p. 79-85.

Blackburn, R. D.; Weldon, L. W. 1962. Control of southern naiad *(Najas guadalupensis)* and other submerged weeds in south Florida irrigation and drainage channels. *Proc. So. Weed Conf.,* vol. 15, p. 254-55.

—. 1963. Suggested control measures for common aquatic weeds of Florida. *Hyacinth Contr. J.,* vol. 2, p. 2-4.

—. 1965. The sensitivity of duckweed *(Lemnaceae)* and azolla to diquat and paraquat. *Weeds,* vol. 13, p. 147-9.

—. 1969. USDA technical report on controlling *Hydrilla verticillata. Weeds, trees and turf,* vol. 8, p. 20-4.

Blackman, G. E. 1960. Responses to environmental factors by plants in the vegetative phase. *Growth of living systems,* p. 525-56. Edited by M. X. Zarrow. New York, Basic Books.

Bock, J. H. 1969. Productivity of the water hyacinth *Eichhornia crassipes* (Mart.) Solms. *Ecology,* vol. 50, p. 460-4.

Bon, C. E.; Lewis, R. H.; Fryer, J. L. 1960. Toxicity of various herbicidal materials to fishes. *Trans. 2nd Semin. Biol. Prob. Water Poll.,* p. 96-101. Cincinnati, Ohio, U.S. Public Health Service.

Boughey, A. S. 1963. The explosive development of a floating weed vegetation on Lake Kariba. *Adansonia,* vol. 3, p. 49-61.

Bowmaker, A. P. 1968. Preliminary observations on some aspects of the biology of the Sinamwenda Estuary, Lake Kariba. *Proc. Trans. Rhod. Scient. Ass.,* vol. 53, p. 3-8.

Boyd, C. E. 1967. Some aspects of aquatic plant ecology. *Reserv. Fish. Resour. Symp., April 5-7, 1967, Athens. Georgia,* p. 114-29. Washington, D.C., Am. Fish. Soc.

—. 1968. Fresh-water plants; a potential source of protein. *Econ. Bot.,* vol. 22, p. 359-68.

—. 1969a. Production, mineral nutrient absorption, and biochemical assimilation by *Justicia americana* and *Alternanthera philoxeroides. Arch. Hydrobiol.,* vol. 66, p. 139-60.

—. 1969b. The nutritive value of three species of water weeds. *Econ. Bot.,* vol. 23, p. 123-7.

—. 1970a. Production, mineral accumulation and pigment concentrations in *Typha latifolia* and *Scirpus americanus. Ecology,* vol. 51, p. 285-90.

—. 1970b. Chemical analyses of some vascular aquatic plants. *Arch. Hydrobiol.,* vol. 67, p. 78-85.

—. 1970c. Vascular aquatic plants for mineral nutrient removal from polluted waters. *Econ. Bot.,* vol. 24, p. 95-103.

—. 1970d. Losses of mineral nutrients during decomposition of *Typha latifolia. Arch. Hydrobiol.,* vol. 66, p. 511-17.

—. 1970e. Amino acid, protein and caloric content of vascular aquatic macrophytes. *Ecology,* vol. 51, p. 902-6.

—. 1971a. The limnological role of aquatic macrophytes and their relationship to reservoir management. *Reservoir fisheries and limnology,* p. 153-66. Edited by G. E. Hall. Washington, D. C., Am. Fish. Soc. (Special pub., no. 8).

—. 1971b. Leaf protein from aquatic plants. *Leaf protein; its agronomy, preparation, quality and use,* p. 44-9. Edited by N. W. Pirie. Oxford, Blackwell (IBP handbook, no. 20).

—. 1972. A bibliography of interest in the utilization of aquatic plants. *Econ. Bot.,* vol. 26.

Boyd, C. E.; Hess, L. W. 1970. Factors influencing shoot production and mineral nutrient levels in *Typha latifolia. Ecology,* vol. 51, p. 296-300.

Bristow, J. M.; Cardenas, J.; Fullerton, T. M.; Sierra, J. 1972. *Malezas aquaticas. Aquatic weeds.* Bogotá (Colombia), Colombian Agricultural Institute, and International Plant Protection Center, Oregon State Univ.

Bruhn, H. D.; Livermore, D. F.; Aboaba, F. O. 1971. Processing characteristics of macrophytes as related to mechanical harvesting. *Trans. Am. Soc. Agric. Engrs,* vol. 14, p. 1004-8.

Bruns, V. F.; Dawson, J. H. 1959. Effects of DCB, DCB-xylene mixtures, amitrol, and sodium salt of dalapon in irrigation water on corn and rutabagas. *Weeds,* vol. 7, p. 333-40.

Bruns, V. F.; Yeo, R. R.; Arle, H. F. 1964. *Tolerance of certain crops to several aquatic herbicides in irrigation water.* 22 p. (U.S. Dep. Agr. tech. bull., 1299).

Burian, K. 1971. Primary production, carbon dioxide exchange and transpiration in *Phragmites communis* Trin. on the Lake Neusiedler See, Austria. *Hidrobiologia,* vol. 12, p. 203-18.

Butcher, R. 1933. Studies on the ecology of rivers. I: On the distribution of macrophytic vegetation in the rivers of Britain. *J. Ecol.,* vol. 21, p. 58-91.

Buttery, B.; Lambert, J. 1965. Competition between *Glyceria maxima* and *Phragmites communis* in the region of Surlingham Broad. I: The competition mechanism. *J. Ecol.* vol. 53, p. 163-81.

Chancellor, R. J.; Coombs, A. V.; Foster, H. S. 1958. Control of aquatic weeds by copper sulfate. *Proc. Brit. Weed Contr. Conf.,* vol. 4, p. 80-4.

Cappleman, L. E.; Sturrock, T. T. 1972. Bacterial,fungal or viral control of aquatic vegetation. Paper presented at the 11th Annual Meeting of the Hyacinth Control Society, Tampa, Fla., July 1971. 4p.

Chapman, V. J. 1970. *History of the lake-weed infestation of the Rotorua Lakes and the lakes of the Waikato hydro-electric system.* 51 p. (N.Z. Dep. Scient. Ind. Res. Inf. Ser., 78).

Chapman, V. J.; Hill, C. F.; Carr, J. L.; Brown, J. M. A. In press. Biology of excessive weed growth in the hydro-electric lakes of the Waikato River, New Zealand. *Int. Symp. Man-made Lakes, Knoxville, Tenn.* Washington, D.C., American Geophysical Union.

Coats, G. E.; Funderburk Jr., H. H.; Lawrence, J. M.; Davis, D. E. 1966. Factors affecting persistence and inactivation of diquat and paraquat. *Weed Res.,* vol. 6, p. 58-66.

Coker, R. E. 1954. *Streams, lakes, ponds.* Chapel Hill, N. C., University of North Carolina Press.

Cook, C. D. K. In preparation. *Water weeds of the world, a manual for the identification of freshwater macrophytes of the world.*

Cook, C. D. K.; Gut, B. J. 1971. *Salvinia* in the state of Kerala, India. *Pestic. Abstr.,* vol. 17, p. 438-47.

Cooper, C. F. 1969. Nutrient output from managed forests. *Eutrophication: causes, consequences, correctives,* p. 446-463. Washington, D.C., National Academy of Sciences.

Coulson, J. R. 1971. Prognosis for control of water hyacinth by arthropods. *Hyacinth Contr. J.,* vol. 9, p. 31-4.

Cowell, B. C. 1965. The effects of sodium arsenite and silvex on the plankton populations in farm ponds. *Trans. Am. Fish. Soc.,* vol. 94, p. 371-7.

Crafts, A. S. 1964. Herbicide behaviour in the plant. In: Audus L. J. (ed.), *The physiology and biochemistry of herbicides.* p. 75-110. New York,Academic Press.

Crance, J. H. 1963. The effects of copper sulfate on *Microcystis* and zooplankton in ponds. *Prog. Fish-Cult.,* vol. 25, p. 198-202.

Crosby, D. G.; Tucker, R. K. 1966. Toxicity of aquatic herbicides to *Daphnia magna. Science,* vol. 154, p. 289-90.

Das, R. R. 1968. Growth and distribution of *Eichhornia crassipes* and *Spirodela polyriza.* Ph. D. thesis, Benares Hindu University.

Datta, S. C.; Biswas, K. K. 1969. Physiology of germination in *Pistia stratiotes* seeds. *Biologia* (Bratislava), vol. 24, p. 70-9.

Dawood, K. I.; Farooq, M.; Dazo, B. C.; Miguel, L. C.; Unrau, G. O. 1965. Herbicide trials in the snail habitats of the Egypt 49 project. *Bull. Wld Hlth. Org.,* vol. 32, p. 269-87.

Dean, J. 1969. *Biology of the crayfish Orconectes causeyi and its use for control of aquatic weeds in trout lakes.* Washington, D.C., Bur. of Sports Fish. and Wildlife (Tech. pap., 24).

Demian, E. S.; Lutfy, R. G. 1964. Prospects of the use of *Marisa cornuarietis* in the biological control of *Limnaea caillaudi* in the UAR. *Proc. Egypt. Acad. Sci.,* vol. 18,, p. 46-50, Pl. I-III.

—. 1965a. Predatory activity of *Marisa cornuarietis* against *Bulinus (Bulinus) truncatus,* the transmitter of urinary schistosomiasis. *Ann. trop. Med. Parasit.,* vol. 59, p. 331-6.

—. 1965b. Predatory activity of *Marisa cornuarietis* against *Biomphalaria alexandrina* under laboratory conditions. *Ann. trop. Med. Parasit.,* vol. 59, p. 337-9.

Demian, E. S.; Ibrahim, A. M. 1969. Feeding activities of the snail *Marisa cornuarietis* (L) under laboratory conditions. *Proc. 6th Arab. Sci. Cong., Damascus, November 1-7, 1969,* part 1, p. 145-65.

Durska, B. 1970. Changes in the reed (*Phragmites communis* Trin.) condition caused by diseases of fungal and animal origin. *Polskie Archwm Hydrobiol.,* vol. 17, p. 373-96.

Dussart, B. 1966. *Limnologie –l'étude des eaux continentales.* Paris, Gauthier-Villars.

Dussart, B. H.; Lagler, K. F.; Larkin, P. A.; Scudder, T.; Szesztay, K.; White, G. F. 1972. *Man-made lakes as modified ecosystems.* Paris, International Council of Scientific Unions. (Scope report, 2).

Edie, H.; Ho, B. 1969. *Ipomoea aquatica* as a vegetable crop in Hong Kong. *Econ. Bot.,* vol. 23, p. 32-6.

Edmondson, W. T. 1970. Phosphorus, nitrogen and algae in Lake Washington after diversion of sewage. *Science* (N.Y.), vol. 169, p. 690-1.

Edwards, R. W.; Brown, M. W. 1960. An aerial photographic method for studying the distribution of aquatic macrophytes in shallow waters. *J. Ecol.,* vol. 48, p. 161-3.

Edwards, D.; Nel, M. D. S. 1972. A reconnaissance survey of aquatic macrophytes in the upper river catchment. *Civ. Engr. S. Afr.,* vol. 14, p. 85-8.

Eipper, A. W. 1959. Effects of five herbicides on farm pond plants and fish. *N. Y. Fish Game J.,* vol. 6, p. 46-56.

Elser, H. J. 1969. Observations on the decline of the water milfoil and other aquatic plants, Maryland, 1962-1967. *Hyacinth Contr. J.,* vol. 8, p. 52-60.

Elton, C. S. 1958. *The ecology of invasions by animals and plants.* London, Methuen.

Evans, J. H. 1961. Growth of Lake Victoria phytoplankton in enriched cultures. *Nature* (Lond.), no. 189, p. 417.

Evans, A. C. 1963. The grip of the water hyacinth. *New Scient.,* vol. 19, p. 666-8.

Evans, G. C. 1972. *The quantitative analysis of plant growth.* Oxford, Blackwell Sci. Publ. 734 p. (Studies in ecology, I).

Falconer, A. F.; Marshall, B. E.; Mitchell, D. S. 1970. Hydrobiological studies of Lake McIlwaine in relation to its pollution, 1968 and 1969. Unpublished report.

Fassett, N. 1969. *A manual of aquatic plants.* Madison, University of Wisconsin Press.

Ferguson, F. F.; Butler, J. M. 1966. Ecology of *Marisa* and its potential as an agent for the elimination of aquatic weeds in Puerto Rico. *Proc. Sth Weed Contr. Conf.* vol. 19, p. 468-76.

Fish, G. R. 1956. Chemical factors limiting growth of phytoplankton in Lake Victoria. *E. Afr. agric. J.,* vol. 21, p. 152-8.

Fisher, R. A. 1920. Some remarks on the methods formulated in a recent article on 'The quantitative analysis of plant growth'. *Ann. appl. Biol.,* vol. 7, p. 367-72.

Flanagan, J. H. 1966. Progress report on use of simazine as an algicide and aquatic herbicide. *Proc. So. Weed Conf.,* vol. 19, p. 387-92.

Forsberg, C. 1959. Quantitative sampling of subaquatic vegetation. *Oikos,* vol. 10, p. 233-40.

—. 1960. Subaquatic macrovegetation in Osbysjon, Djussholm. *Oikos,* vol. 11, p. 183-99.

Frank, P. A. 1966. Persistence and distribution of monuron and neburon in an aquatic environment. *Weed,* vol. 14, p. 219-22.

Franz, T.; Cordone, A. 1967. Observations on deepwater plants in Lake Tahoe, California and Nevada. *Ecology,* vol. 48, p. 709-14.

Funderburk, Jr. H.H.; Lawrence, J. M. 1964. Mode of action and metabolism of diquat and paraquat. *Weeds,* vol. 12, p. 259-64.

Funderburk, Jr., H.H.; Negi, N. S.; Lawrence, J. M. 1966. Photochemical decomposition of diquat and paraquat. *Weeds,* vol. 14, p. 240-3.

Gajevskaya, N. S. 1966. *The role of higher aquatic plants in the nutrition of the animals of fresh-water basins.* 3 vols. Russian original: Moscow, 1966, 629 p. Translation: Dr. D. G. Maitland Muller, Dr. K. H. Mann (ed.), National Lending Library for Science and Technology, 1969.

Gaudet, J. J. In press. Standardised growth conditions for an aquatic weed, *Salvinia. Hydrobiologia.*

Gay, P. A. 1960. The water hyacinth and the Sudan. *The biology of weeds,* p. 184-8. Edited by J. L. Harper. Oxford, Blackwell.

Gessner, F. 1955. *Hydrobotanik: die physiologischen Grundlagen der Pflanzenverbreitung im Wasser. I: Energiehaushalt.* Berlin, VEB Deutscher Verlag der Wissenschaften.

—. 1959. *Hydrobotanik: die physiologischen Grundlagen der Pflanzenverbreitung im Wasser. II: Stoffhaushalt.* Berlin, VEB Deutscher Verlag der Wissenschaften.

Gilderhus, P. A. 1967. Effects of diquat on bluegills and their food organisms. *Prog. Fish-Cult.,* vol. 29, p. 67-74.

Golterman, H. L.; Clymo, R. S. 1971. *Methods for chemical analysis of fresh waters.* Oxford, Blackwell. (IBP handbook, no. 8).

Gopal, B. 1967. Contribution of *Azolla pinnata* R. Br. to the productivity of temporary ponds at Varanasi. *Trop. Ecol.,* vol. 8, p. 126-30.

Gorham, E. 1953. Chemical studies on the soils and vegetation of waterlogged habitats in the English Lake District. *J. Ecol.,* vol. 41, p. 345-60.

Gupta, R. S. 1966. A study of hydrophytes and marsh plants of Kota and environs (India). *Trop. Ecol.,* vol. 7, p. 153-61.

Guscio, F. J.; Bartley, T. R.; Beck, A. N. 1965. Water resources problems generated by obnoxious plants. *J. Watways Harb. Div. Am. Soc. Civ. Engrs.,* vol. 10, p. 47-60.

Hall, J. B.; Laing, E.; Hossain, M.; Lawson, G. W. 1969. Observations on aquatic weeds in the Volta Basin. *Man-made lakes. The Accra symposium,* p. 331-43. Edited by L. E. Obeng. Accra, Ghana Universities Press.

Hammerton, J. L.; Stone, M. 1966. Studies on weed species of the genus *Polygonum* 2: Physiological variation within *P. lapathifolium. Weed. Res.,* vol. 6, p. 104-31.

Harrison, D. S.; Blackburn, R. D.; Weldon, L. W.; Orsenigo, J. R.; Ryan, G. F. 1966. *Aquatic weed control.* 16 p. (Florida Agr. Ext. Serv. circ., 219B).

Haslam, S. M. 1968. The biology of reed *(Phragmites communis)* in relation to its control. *Proc. 9th Brit. Weed Contr. Conf.,* p. 392-7.

—. 1970*a*. Variation of population type in *Phragmites communis* Trin. *Ann. Bot.,* vol. 34, p. 147-58.

—. 1970*b*. The performance of *Phragmites communis* Trin. in relation to water-supply. *Ann. Bot.,* vol. 34, p. 867-77.

—. 1971*a*. The development and establishment of young plants of *Phragmites communis* Trin. *Ann. Bot.,* vol. 35, p. 1059-72.

—. 1971*b*. Physical factors and some river weeds. *Proc. Eur. Weed Res. Coun. 3rd Int. Symp. Aquat. Weeds 1971,* p. 29-39.

Herzog, R. 1935. Ein Beitrag zur Systematik der Gattung *Salvinia. Hedwigia,* vol. 74, p. 257-84.

Hesse, P. 1957. The distribution of sulphur in the muds, water and vegetation of Lake Victoria. *Hydrobiologia,* vol. 11, p. 29-39.

Hesse, P. 1958. Fixation of sulphur in the muds of Lake Victoria. *Hydrobiologia.* vol. 11, p. 171-81.

Hickling, C. F. 1965. Biological control of aquatic vegetation. *Pestic. Abstr.,* vol. 11, p. 237-44.

Hiltibran, R. C. 1962. Duration of toxicity of endothall in water. *Weeds,* vol. 10, p. 17-19.

Hitchcock, A. E.; Zimmerman, P. W.; Kirkpatrick, H.; Earle, T. T. 1949. Water hyacinth: its growth, reproduction, and practical control by 2, 4-D. *Contr. Boyce Thomson Inst. Pl. Res.,* vol. 15, p. 363-401.

Holm, L. G.; Weldon, L. W.; Blackburn, R. D. 1969. Aquatic weeds. *Science* (N.Y.) vol. 166, p. 699-709.

Holm, L. G.; Herberger, J. 1971. World list of useful publications for the study of weeds and their control. *Pestic. Abstr.,* vol. 17. Suppl.,14 p.

Howard-Williams, C.; Furse, M.; Schulten-Senden, C.; Bourn, D.; Lenton, G. 1972. *Lake Chilwa, Malawi. Studies on a tropical freshwater ecosystem.* Report to IBP/UNESCO Symposium, Reading (England).

Hoogers, B. J.; van der Weij. H. G. The development cycle of some aquatic plants in the Netherlands. *Proc. Eur. Weed Res. Coun. 3rd Int. Symp. Aquat. Weeds, 1971,* p. 3-18.

Houser, A.; Gaylor, J. Y. 1961. Initial results of silvex in seven Oklahoma ponds. *Proc. So: Weed Conf.,* vol. 14, p. 295-8.

Hubbard, J.; Stebbings, R. 1968. *Spartina* marshes in southern England. VII: Stratigraphy of the Keysworth Marsh, Poole Harbour. *J. Ecol.,* vol. 56, p. 707-22.

Huckins, R. K. 1955. Aquatic weed control studies in New Jersey. A progress report. *Proc. No. East. Contr. Conf.* vol. 9, p. 519-34.

—. 1960. Aquatic weed control, Carnegie Lake, Princeton, New Jersey. *Proc. No. East Weed Contr. Conf.,* vol. 14, p. 496-501.

Hughes, H. R. 1971. Control of the water weed problem in the Rerva River. *Fiji Agric. J.,* vol. 33, p. 67-72.

Hutchinson, G. E. 1957. *A treatise on limnology.* Vol. I: *Geography, physics and chemistry.* New York, John Wiley & Sons Inc.

—. 1967. *A treatise on limnology.* Vol. II: *Introduction to lake biology and the limnoplankon.* New York, John Wiley & Sons Inc.

—. 1969. Eutrophication, past and present. *Eutrophication: causes, consequences, correctives,* p. 17-26. Washington, D.C., National Academy of Sciences.

Hynes, H. 1959. The biological effects of water pollution. *The effects of pollution on living material*, p. 11-24. Edited by W. B. Yapp. London, Institute of Biology.

Hynes, H. 1960. *The biology of polluted waters.* Liverpool, Liverpool University Press.

Hynes, H. 1970. *The ecology of running waters.* Liverpool, Liverpool University Press.

Jackson, D. F. 1967. *Interaction between algal populations and viruses in model pools —a possible control for algal blooms.* Presented at ASCE Annual and National Meeting on Water Resources Engineering, Statler Hilton, New York, 1967.

Jewell, W. J. 1970. Aquatic weed decay: dissolved oxygen utilization and nitrogen and phosphorus regeneration. *43rd a. Conf. Wat. Pollut. Contr., Boston.*

Jordan, P.; Webbe, G. 1969. *Human schistosomiasis.* London, William Heinemann Medical Books Ltd.

Junk, W. 1970. Investigations on the ecology and production-biology of the "floating meadows" (Paspalo-Echinochloetum) on the Middle Amazon. Part I: The floating vegetation and its ecology. *Amazoniana*, vol. 11: 449-495.

Keckemet, Obren. 1969. Chemical, toxicological, and biological properties of endothall. *Hyacinth Contr. J.,* vol. 8, p. 50-1.

King, L. J. 1966. *Weeds of the world. Biology and control.* New York, Interscience Publishers Inc.

King, D. L. 1970. The role of carbon in eutrophication. *J. Wat. Pollut. Contr. Fed.,* vol. 42, p. 2035-51.

Klingman, G. C. 1961. *Weed control: as a science.* New York, John Wiley & Sons Inc., 421 p.

Krupauer, V. 1971. The use of herbivorous fishes for ameliorative purposes in Central and Eastern Europe. *Proc. Eur. Weed Res. Coun. 3rd Int. Symp. Aquat. Weeds 1971,* p. 95-103.

Lagler, K. F. (ed.) 1969. *Man-made lakes—planning and development.* Rome, Food and Agriculture Organization of the United Nations.

Lambert, J. 1946. The distribution and status of *Glyceria maxima* (Hartm.) Holmb. in the region of Surlingham and Rockland Broads, Norfolk. *J. Ecol.,* vol. 33, p. 230-67.

Laundon, G. F.; Ponnappa, K. M. 1966. A new species of *Vredo* on *Hygrophila. Curr. Sci.,* vol. 19, p. 492-3.

Lawrence, J. M. 1962. *Aquatic herbicide data.* 133 p. (Agricultural handbook, no. 231).

Lawrence, J. M.; Blackburn, R. D. 1963. Status of diquat and paraquat as aquatic herbicides. *Proc. Conf. Southeastern Assoc. Game & Fish Comm.,* vol. 16, p. 157-63.

Lawson, M. A.; Barnes, W. W.; Harris, F. W.; Nelson, L. L. 1970. *Bioassay of herbicide-impregnated polyvinyl chloride pellets for the control of eurasian watermilfoil (Myriophyllum spicatum).* (Weed Science Society Abstracts, no. 9).

Lebrun, J. 1959. La lutte contre le développement de l'*Eichhornia crassipes. Bull. agric. Congo Belge,* vol. 50, p. 251-2.

Lekic, M. 1970. Ecology of the aquatic insect species *Paraponyx stratiotata* L. (Pyraustidae, Lepidoptera). *Arh. poljopr. Nauke Teh.,* vol. 23, p. 49-62.

Lekic, M.; Mihajlovic, L. 1970. Entomofauna of *Myriophyllum spicatum* L. (Halorrhagidaceae), an aquatic weed on Yugoslav territory. *Arch. poljopr. Nauke Teh.,* vol. 23, p. 63-76.

Liebmann, H. 1960. *Handbuch der Frischwasser und Abwasserbiologie,* Vol. II. München, R. Oldenbourg.

——. 1962. *Handbuch der Frischwasser und Abwasserbiologie.* Vol. I. München. R. Oldenbourg.

Linacre, E. T.; Hicks, B. B.; Sainty, G. R.; Grauze, G. 1970. The evaporation from a swamp. *Agr. Meteorol.,* vol. 7, p. 375-86.

Little, E. C. S. 1966. The invasion of man-made lakes by plants. *Man-made lakes,* p. 75-86. Edited by R. H. Lowe-McConnell. London, Academic Press.

——. 1967. Progress report on transpiration of some tropical water weeds. *Pestic. Abstr.,* vol. 13, p. 127-32.

——. 1968. The control of water weeds. *Weed Res.,* vol. 8, p. 75-105.

——. 1969. Weeds and man-made lakes. *Man-made lakes. The Accra symposium,* p. 284-91. Edited by L. E. Obeng. Accra, Ghana Universities Press.

Little, E. C. S. (ed.) 1968. *Handbook of utilization of aquatic plants.* Rome, Food and Agriculture Organization of the United Nations.

Livermore, D. F.; Wunderlich, W. E. 1969. Mechanical removal of organic production from waterways. *Eutrophication: causes, consequences, correctives,* p. 494-519. Washington, D.C., National Academy of Sciences.

Low, J. B.; Bellrose, F. C. 1944. The seed and vegetative yield of waterfowl food plants in the Illinois River valley. *J. Wildl. Mgmt.,* vol. 8, p. 7-22.

Lowe-McConnel, R. H. (ed.) 1966. *Man-made lakes.* London, Academic Press.

Loyal, D. S.; Grewal, R. K. 1966. Cytological study on sterility in *Salvinia auriculata* Aublet with a bearing on its reproductive mechanism. *Cytologia,* vol. 31, p. 330-8.

Lund, J. W. G. 1969. Phytoplankton. *Eutrophication: causes, consequences, correctives,* p. 306-30. Washington, D.C., National Academy of Sciences.

Mackenthum, K. M. 1950. Aquatic weed control with sodium arsenite. *Sewage Ind. Wastes,* vol. 22, p. 8.

Mackenthum, Kenneth; Ingram, W. M.; Porges, R. 1964. Limnological aspects of recreational lakes. Washington, D. C., U.S. Govt. Printing Office. 176 p. (U.S. Public Health Service pub., no. 1167).

Mackenthum, K. M. 1965. *Nitrogen and phosphorus in water—an annotated selected bibliography of their biological effects.* Washington, D.C., U.S. Dept. of Health, Education and Welfare, U.S. Govt. Printing Office.

Mackenzie, J. W.; Hall, L. 1967. Elodea control in southeast Florida with diquat. *Hyacinth Contr. J.,* vol. 6, p. 37-44.

Mackereth, F. J. H. 1963. *Some methods of water analysis for limnologists.* (Freshwater Biological Association Scientific Publication, 21).

McLachlan, A. J. 1969. The effect of aquatic macrophytes on the variety and abundance of benthic fauna in a newly created lake in the tropics (Lake Kariba). *Arch. Hydrobiol.,* vol. 66, p. 212-31.

McNabb, C. D.; Tiernay, D. P.; Kosek, S. R. 1971. *The uptake of phosphorus by Ceratophyllum demersum from waste water.* Project A-031-Mich of the Inst. Wat. Research, Michigan State Univ.

Maddox, D. M.; Andres, L. A.; Hennessey, R. D.; Blackburn, R. D.; Spencer, N. R. 1971. Insects to control alligatorweed: an invader of aquatic ecosystems in the United States. *Bioscience,* vol. 21, p. 985-91.

Maestri, M. 1967. Structural and functional effects of endothall on plants. 122 p. Thesis, University of California.

Mahal, M. S. 1969. Aquatic weeds and their control. *Man-made lakes. The Accra symposium,* p. 337-43. Edited by L. E. Obeng. Accra, Ghana Universities Press.

Malony, T. E.; Miller, W.E.; Blind, N. L. 1972. Use of algal assays in studying eutrophication problems. 10 p. Paper presented at 6th Int. Wat. Pollut. Research.

Martin, J. B.; Bradford, B. N.; Kennedy, H. G. 1970. Relationship of nutritional and environmental factors to selected rooted aquatic macrophytes. Part I: Factors affecting growth of *Najas* in Pickwick Reservoir. *TVA activities related to study and control of eutrophication in the Tennessee Valley.* Alabama, National Fertilizer Development Center, Musele Shoals.

— . In press. Nutritional studies with *Najas sp. Int. Symp. Man-made Lakes, Knoxville, Tenn.* Washington, D.C., American Geophysical Union.

Mason, R. 1960. Three waterweeds of the family Hydrocharitaceae in New Zealand. *N.Z. J. Sci.,* vol. 3, p. 382-95.

Massini, P. 1961. The movement of 2,6-dichlorobenzonitrile in soils and plants in relation to its physical properties. *Weed Res.,* vol. 1, p. 142-6.

Mehta, I.; Sharma, R. K. 1972. Control of aquatic weeds by the White Amur in Rajasthan, India. *Hyacinth Contr. J.,* vol. 10, p. 16-19.

Michewicz, J. E.; Sutton, D. L.; Blackburn, R. D. 1972*a.* The White Amur for aquatic weed control. *Weed Sci.,* vol. 20, p. 106-10.

—. 1972*b.* Water quality of small enclosures stocked with white amur. *Hyacinth Contr. J.,* vol. 10, p. 22-5.

Milner, C.; Hughes, R. E. 1968. *Methods for the measurement of the primary production of grassland.* Oxford, Blackwell. (IBP handbook, no. 8).

Mitchell, D. S. 1965. Research on *Salvinia auriculata. Lake Kariba Fish. Res. Inst. Symp., Kariba, June, 1965,* p. 51-6 (cyclostyled).

—. 1969. The ecology of vascular hydrophytes on Lake Kariba. *Hydrobiologia,* vol. 34, p. 448-64.

—. 1970. Autecological studies of *Salvinia auriculata.* Ph.D. thesis, University of London.

— . In press *a.* Aquatic weeds in man-made lakes. *Int. Symp. Man-made Lakes, Knoxville, Tenn.* Washington, D. C. American Geophysical Union.

—. In press *b. Salvinia molesta* sp. nov. *Br. Fern Gaz.*

Mitchell, D. S.; Thomas, P. A. 1972. *Ecology of water weeds in the neotropics.* Paris, Unesco, (Technical papers in hydrology, no. 12).

Mitchell, D. S.; Tur, N. M. In preparation. The rate of growth of *Salvinia molesta (S. auriculata* Auct.) in laboratory and natural conditions.

Moore, G. T.; Kellerman, K. R. 1904. *Methods of destroying or preventing growth of algae in water supplies.* 44 p. (U.S. Dep. Agr. Bur. Plant Industry Bull., 64).

Moreland, D. E.; Gentner, W. A.; Hilton J. L.; Hill, K. L. 1959. Studies on the mechanism of herbicidal action of 2-chloro-4,6 bis (ethylamino)-s-triazine. *Plant. Physiol.,* vol. 34, p. 432-5.

Morrison, F. B. 1961. *Feeds and feeding, abridged.* Clinton, Iowa, The Morrison Publ. Co.

Mortimer, C. H. 1941. The exchange of dissolved substances between mud and water in lakes, I and II. *J. Ecol.,* vol. 29, p. 280-329.

——. 1942. The exchange of dissolved substances between mud and water in lakes, III and IV. *J. Ecol.,* vol. 30, p. 147-201.

Moss, B. 1969. Limitation of algal growth in some Central African waters. *Limnol. Oceanogr.,* vol. 14, p. 591-601.

Mulligan, H. F. 1969. Management of aquatic vascular plants and algae. *Eutrophication: causes, consequences, correctives,* p. 464-82. Washington, D.C., National Academy of Sciences.

Mulligan, H.; Baranowski, A. 1969. Growth of phytoplankton and vascular aquatic plants at different nutrient levels. *Verh. int. Verein theor. angew. Limnol.,* vol. 17, p. 802-10.

Muirhead-Thomson, R. C. 1971. *Pesticides and freshwater fauna.* London and New York Academic Press.

Nag Raj, T. R. 1965. Thread blight of water hyacinth. *Curr. Sci.,* vol. 34, p. 618-19.

——. 1966. Fungi occurring on witchweed in India. *Tech. Bull. Commonw. Inst. Biol. Contr.,* vol. 7, p. 75-79.

Nag Raj, T. R.; Ponnappa, K. M. 1970a. Some interesting fungi occurring on aquatic weeds and *Striga* spp. in India. *J. Indian Bot. Soc.,* vol. 49, p. 64-71.

——. 1970b. Blight of water hyacinth caused by *Alternaria eichhorniae* sp. nov. *Trans. Br. Mycol. Soc.,* vol. 55, p. 123-30.

National Academy of Sciences. 1969. *Eutrophication: causes, consequences, correctives.* Washington, D.C.

Neel, J. K. 1963. Impact of reservoirs. *Limnology in North America,* p. 575-93. Edited by D. G. Frey. Madison, Univ. of Wisconsin Press.

Nelson, J. L.; Bruns, V. F.; Coutant, C. C.; Carlile, B. L. 1969. Behaviour and reactions of copper sulfate in an irrigation canal. *Pesticides Monitoring J.,* vol. 3, p. 186-9.

Nye, P. H.; Greenland, D. J. 1960. *The soil under shifting cultivation.* Farnham Royal, Bucks. (England), Commonw. Bur. Soils. Commonw. Agric. Bur. (Tech. Comm. 51).

Nygaard, G. 1958. On the productivity of the bottom vegetation in Lake Grane, Langsø. *Verh. int. Verein theor. angew. Limnol.,* vol. 13, p. 144-55.

Obeng, L. E. (ed.). 1969. *Man-made lakes. The Accra symposium.* Accra, Ghana Universities Press.

Odum, H. T. 1957. Trophic structure and productivity of Silver Springs, Florida. *Ecol. Monogr.,* vol. 27, p. 55-112.

Oliver-Gonzales, J.; Baumar, P. N.; Benenson, A. S. 1956. Effect of the snail *Marisa cornuarietis* on *Australorbis glabratus* in natural bodies of water in Puerto Rico. *Am. J. trop. Med. Hyg.,* vol. 5, p. 290-6.

Ophel, I.; Fraser C. 1970. Calcium and strontium discrimination by aquatic plants. *Ecology,* vol. 51, p. 324-7.

Parsons, W. T. 1963. Water hyacinth. A pest of world waterways. *J. Agric. Vict. Dep. Agric.,* vol. 9, p. 23-7.

Pearsall, W. H. 1920. The aquatic vegetation of the English lakes. *J. Ecol.,* vol. 8, p. 163-201.

——. 1921. The development of vegetation in the English lakes, considered in relation to the general evolution of glacial lakes and rock-basins. *Proc. R. Soc.,* Ser. B, vol. 92, p. 259-84.

Peltier, W. H.; Welch, E. B. 1969. Factors affecting growth of rooted aquatics in a river. *Weed Sci.,* vol. 17, p. 412-16.

——. 1970. Factors affecting growth of rooted aquatic plants in a reservoir. *Weed Sci.,* vol. 18, p. 7-9.

Penfound, W. T. 1956. Primary production of vascular aquatic plants. *Limnol. Oceanogr.,* vol. 1, p. 92-101.

Penfound, W. T.; Earle, T. T. 1948. The biology of the water hyacinth. *Ecol. Monogr.,* vol. 18, p. 447-72.

Penfound, W. T.; Hall, T. F.; Hess, A. D. 1945. The spring phenology of plants in and around the reservoirs in North Alabama with particular reference to malaria control. *Ecology,* vol. 26, p. 332-52.

Penman, H. L. 1963. *Vegetation and hydrology.* Farnham Royal, Bucks. (England), Commonw. Bur. Soils, Commonw. Agric. Bur. (Tech. Comm. 53).

Percival, E.; Whitehead, H. 1929. A quantitative study of some types of stream-bed. *J. Ecol.*, vol. 17, p. 282-314.

Petr, T. 1968. Population changes in aquatic invertebrates living on two water plants in a tropical man-made lake. *Hydrobiologia*, vol. 32, p. 449-85.

—. 1970. Macroinvertebrates of flooded trees in the man-made Volta Lake (Ghana) with special reference to the burrowing may fly, *Povilla adusta* Navas. *Hydrobiologia*, vol. 36, p. 373-98.

Pettet, A. 1964. Seedlings of *Eichhornia crassipes* : a possible complication to control measures in the Sudan. *Nature* (Lond.), no. 201, p. 516-17.

Pettet, A.; Pettet, S. J. 1970. Biological control of *Pistia stratiotes* L. in Western State, Nigeria. *Nature* (Lond.), no. 226, p. 282.

Phillipson, J. 1966. *Ecological energetics.* London, Edward Arnold (Publishers) Ltd.

Pirie, N. W. 1971. Equipment and methods for extracting and separating protein. *Leaf protein: its agronomy, preparation, quality and use*, p. 53-62. Edited by N. W. Pirie. Oxford, Blackwell. (IBP handbook, no. 20).

Planter, M. 1970. Elution of mineral components out of dead reed, *Phragmites communis* Trin. *Polskie Archwm. Hydrobiol.*, vol. 17, p. 357-62.

Polisini, J. M.; Boyd, C. E. 1972. Relationships between cell-wall fractions, nitrogen, and standing crop in aquatic macrophytes. *Ecology*, vol. 53, p. 484-8.

Ponnappa, K. M. 1970. On the pathogenicity of *Myrothecium roridum-Eichhornia crassipes* isolate. *Hyacinth Contr. J.*, vol. 8, p. 18-20.

Prowse, G. A. 1964. Some limnological problems in tropical fish ponds. *Verh. int. Verein theor. angew. Limnol.*, vol. 15, p. 400-4.

Prowse, G. A.; Talling, J. F. 1958. The seasonal growth and succession of plankton algae in the White Nile. *Limnol. Oceanogr.*, vol. 3, p. 222-38.

Radford, P. J. 1967. Growth analysis formulae—their use and abuse. *Crop. Sci.*, vol. 7, p. 171-5.

Rao, V. P. 1965. Survey for natural enemies of witchweed and water hyacinth and other aquatic weeds affecting waterways in India: Report for the period January to December 1964. Commonw. Inst. Biol. Control (Unpublished report).

—. 1969. Possibilities of biological control of aquatic weeds in India. *Water Resour. J.*, vol. 82, p. 40-50.

Ranwell, D. S. 1964. *Spartina* salt marshes in southern England. II: Rate and seasonal pattern of sediment accretion. *J. Ecol.*, vol. 52, p. 79-94.

—. 1967. Introduced aquatic, fresh-water and salt marsh plants—case histories and ecological effects. *Proc. IUCN 10th Tech. Meeting (Lucerne, 1966)*, p. 27-37 (IUCN Publ., New ser., no. 9).

Reid, G. K. 1961. *Ecology of inland waters and estuaries.* New York, Reinhold Publ. Corp.

Rich, P. 1970. Utilization of benthic detritus in a marl lake. Ph. D. thesis, Michigan State University.

Rich, E. R.; Rouse, W. 1970. Mass producing a tropical snail for biological control. *Proc. Sth Weed Control Conf.*, vol. 23, p. 288-98.

Riemer, D. N.; Toth, S. J. 1968. *A survey of the chemical composition of aquatic plants in New Jersey* (New Jers. Agric. Exp. Sta. Bull., 80).

—. 1969. A survey of the chemical composition of *Potamogeton* and *Myriophyllum* in New Jersey. *Weed Sci.*, vol. 17, p. 219-23.

—. 1970. Chemical composition for species of Nymphaeaceae. *Weed Sci.*, vol. 18, p. 4-6.

Rijks, D. A. 1969. Evaporation from a papyrus swamp. *Q. J. R. Met. Soc.*, vol. 95, p. 643-9.

Robson, T. O. 1967. *A survey of the problem of aquatic weed control in England and Wales.* 27 p. (ARC Weed Res. Org. Tech. Rept., no. 5).

Robson, T. O. 1968. *The control of aquatic weeds.* London (England) (Ministry of Agr. Fish and Food Bull., no. 194).

Rozeboom, L. E.; Hess, A. D. 1944. The relation of the intersection line to the production of *Anopheles quadrimaculatus*. *J. Natn. Malar. Soc.*, vol. 3, p. 169-81. Cited by Penfound, Hall & Hess (1945).

Rudescu, L.; Niculescu, C.; Chivu, I. P. 1965. *Monografia stufului den delta Dunarii.* Romania, Editura Academiei Republicii Socialiste.

Russel-Hunter, W. D. 1970. *Aquatic productivity.* New York, Macmillan.

Ruttner, F. 1963. *Fundamentals of liminology.* Toronto, University of Toronto Press.

Safferman, R. S.; Morris, M. E. 1967. Observations on the occurence, distribution and seasonal incidence of blue-green algae viruses. *Appl. Microbiol.*, vol. 15, p. 1219-22.

Sanders, H. O.; Cope, O. B. 1966. Toxicity of several pesticides to two species of cladocerans. *Trans. Amer. Fish. Soc.,* vol. 95, p. 165-9.

Sankaran, T.; Srinath, D.; Krishna, K. 1966. Studies on *Gesonula punctifrons* Stal. (Orthoptera: Acrididae: Cyrtacanthacridinae) attacking water hyacinth in India. *Entomophaga.,* vol. 11, p. 433-40.

Sankaran, T.; Menon, P. K. B.; Narayanan, E.; Krishna, K.; Ranganath Bhat, Y. 1970. Studies on natural enemies of witchweed, nutsedge and several aquatic weeds (for USA). *Commonw. Inst. Biol. Contr. a.Rep. 1971.*

Sankaran, T.; Rao, V. P.; Narayanan, E.; Ramaseshiah, G.; Krishaswamy, S.; Krishna, K. 1971. Studies on natural enemies of witchweed, nutsedge and water hyacinth and several other aquatic weeds (for USA and Zambia). *Commonw. Inst. Biol. Contr. a. Rep. 1971.*

Schuster, W. H. 1952. Fish culture as a means of controlling aquatic weeds in inland waters. *Fish. Bull. F.A.O.,* vol. 5, p. 15-24.

Schwoerbel, J. 1966. *Methoden der Hydrobiologie-Kosmos.* Stuttgart, Gesellschaft der Naturfreunde Franckh'sche Verlagshandlung.

Sculthorpe, C. D. 1967. *The biology of aquatic vascular plants.* London, Edward Arnold (Publishers) Ltd.

Seaman, D. E.; Porterfield, W. A. 1964. Control of aquatic weeds by the snail, *Marisa cornuarietis. Weeds,* vol. 12, p. 87-92.

Seaman, D. E.; Thomas, T. M. 1966. Translocation of herbicides in American pondweed. *Weed Sci. Soc. Abstr.,* p. 65.

Seidel, K. 1971. Macrophytes as functional elements in the environment of man. *Hidrobiologia,* vol. 12, p. 121-30.

Sestak, Z.; Catsky, J.; Jarvis, P. G. (eds.). 1971. *Plant photosynthetic production. Manual of methods.* The Hague, Junk, 818 p.

Sguros, P. L.; Monkus, T.; Phillips, C. 1965. Observations and techniques in the study of the Florida manatee—reticent, but superb weed control agent. *Proc. Sth Weed Control Conf.,* vol. 18, p. 588.

Sharma, A. 1971. Eradication and utilisation of water hyacinth—a review. *Curr. Sci.,* vol. 40, p. 51-5.

Sheffield, C. W. 1967. Water hyacinth for nutrient removal. *Hyacinth Contr. J.,* vol. 6, p. 27-31.

Silva, L. de Olivieri de. 1960. Control biologico de *Anacharis densa* (Planch.) Vict., nos lagos de Universidad Rural de Rio de Janeiro. *Agronomia Rio de J.,* vol. 18, p. 117-27.

Singh, S.B. 1962. Preliminary experiments on the relative manurial values of some aquatic weeds as composts. *Handbook of utilization of aquatic plants,* p. 82-86. Edited by E. C. S. Little. Rome, Food and Agriculture Organization of the United Nations.

Sioli, H. 1968. Principal biotopes of primary production in the waters of Amazonia. *Proc. Symp. Recent Adv. Trop. Ecol.,* p. 591-600.

Smalley, A. 1960. Energy flow of a salt marsh grasshopper population. *Ecology,* vol. 41, p. 672-7.

Smirnov, N. 1961. Consumption of emergent plants by insects. *Verh. int. Verein theor. angew. Limnol.,* vol. 14, p. 232-6.

Smith, N. W. 1935. The use of copper sulfate for eradicating the predatory fish population of a lake. *Trans. Amer. Fish. Soc.,* vol. 65, p. 101-14.

—. 1939. Copper sulfate and rotenone as fish poisons. *Trans. Amer. Fish. Soc.,* vol. 69, p. 141-57.

Snow, J. R. 1973. Simazine as an algicide for bass ponds. *Prog. Fish-Cult.,* vol. 25, p. 34-6.

—. 1956. Algae control in warm-water hatchery ponds. *Proc. Conf. Southeast Assoc. Game Commrs.,* vol. 10, p. 80-4.

Southern Weed Conference. 1960. Project (4) Aquatic Weeds. *Proc. So. Weed Conf.* vol. 13, p. 367-89.

Spence, D. 1967. Factors controlling the distribution of freshwater macrophytes with particular reference to the lochs of Scotland. *J. Ecol.,* vol. 55, p. 147-70.

Spencer, N. R. 1971. The potential usefulness of an aquatic Lepidoptera as a control agent for *Myriophyllum spicatum. Proc. Sth Weed Contr. Conf.,* vol. 24, p. 348.

Starr, T.; Jones, M.; Martinez, D. 1957. The production of vitamin B_{12}-active substances by marine bacteria. *Limnol. Oceanogr.,* vol. 2, p. 114-19.

Steenis, J. H.; Lawrence, P. S.; Cofer, H. P. 1959. Studies on cattail management in the North-East. *Trans. 10th NE Wildl. Conf.* (1958, Montreal), p. 149-55.

Stott, B.; Cross, D. G.; Iszard, R. E.; Robson, T. O. 1971. Recent work on grasscarp in the United Kingdom from the standpoint of its economics in controlling submerged aquatic plants. *Proc. Eur. Weed Res. Coun. 3rd Int. Symp. Aquat. Weeds 1971,* p. 105-16.

Straskraba, M. 1968. Der Anteil der Höheren Pflanzen and der Produktion der Stehenden Gewässer. In: W. van Ohle, (ed.), Stoffhaushalt der Binnengewässer, Chemie und Mikrobiologie, *Mitt. int. Verein. theor. angew. Limnol.*, vol. 14, p. 212-30.

Strickland, J. D. H.; Parsons, T. R. 1965. *Bull. 125 of the Fish. Res. Board of Canada.* 2nd rev. ed. Ottawa.

Surber, E. W. 1943. Weed control in hard-water ponds with copper sulfate and sodium arsenite. *Trans. North Amer. Wildlife Conf.*, vol. 8, p. 132-41.

——. 1949. *Control of aquatic plants in ponds and lakes.* 20 p.(U.S. Dep. of Interior, Fish and Wildlife Service, Fishery Leafl., no. 344).

——. 1961. *Improving sport fishing by control of aquatic weeds.* Washington, D.C., U. S. Government Printing Office, 37 p. (Dep. of Interior Circ., 128).

Surber, E. W.; Pickering, Q. H. 1962. Acute toxicity of endothall,diquat, hyamine, dalapon, and silvex to fish. *Prog. Fish-Cult.*, vol. 24, p. 164-71.

Sutton, D. L.; Bingham, S. W. 1968. Translocation patterns of simazine in *Potamogeton crispus* L. *Proc. No. East. Weed Contr. Conf.*, vol. 22, p. 357-61.

——. 1969. Absorption and translocation of simazine in parrotfeather. *Weed Sci.*, vol. 17, p. 431-5.

——. 1970. Uptake and translocation of 2,4-D-1-^{14}C in parrotfeather. *Weed Sci.*, vol. 18, p. 193-6.

Sutton, D. L.; Evrard, T. D.; Chappell, W. E. 1965. Effects of simazine on aquatic plants in a farm pond. *Proc. No. East. Weed Contr. Conf.*, vol. 19, p. 440-4.

Sutton, D. L.; Evrard, T. O.; Bingham, S. W. 1966. The effects of repeated treatments of simazine on certain aquatic plants and residue in water. *Proc. No. East. Weed Contr. Conf.*, vol. 20, p.. 464-8.

Sutton, D. L.; Weldon, L. W.; Blackburn, R. D. 1970. Effect of diquat on the uptake of copper in aquatic plants. *Proc. So. Weed Sci. Soc.*, vol. 18, p. 703-7.

Sutton, D. L.; Durham, D. A.; Bingham, S. W.; Foy, C. L. 1969. Influence of simazine on apparent photosynthesis of aquatic plants and herbicide residue removal from water. *Weed Sci.*, vol. 17, p. 56-9.

Swingle, H. S. 1957. Control of pond weeds by the use of herbivorous fishes. *Proc. Sth Weed Control Conf.*, vol. 10, p. 11-17.

Symposium: the aquatic environment and man. *Proc. R. Soc. Vict.*, vol. 83, 1969, p. 1-54.

Talling, J. F. 1965. Productivity of phytoplankton in Lake Victoria. *J. appl. Ecol.*, vol. 2, p. 415 (Abstract only).

——. 1966. Comparative problems of phytoplankton production and photosynthetic productivity in a tropical and a temperate lake. *Primary productivity in aquatic environments*, p. 399-424. Edited by C. Goldman. Berkeley, University of California Press. (Mem. 1st Ital. Idrobiol., 18 (suppl.).)

Taylor, James L. 1966. Casoron, a new aquatic herbicide. *Hyacinth Contr. J.*, vol. 5, p. 20-1.

——. 1968. Control of spatterdock with casoron. *Hyacinth. Contr. J.*, vol. 7, p. 40-1.

Templeton, R. G. 1971. Aquatic weed control with polythene sheeting. *J. Inst. Fish Mgmt*, vol. 3, p. 18-19.

Thomas, E. A. 1969. The process of eutrophication in Central European lakes. *Eutrophication: causes, consequences, correctives*, p. 29-49. Washington, D.C., National Academy of Sciences.

Thomas, T. M. 1966. Uptake and fate of endothall in submerged aquatic plants. 105 p. Thesis, Univ. of California.

Thomas, T. M.; Seaman, D. E. 1968. Translocation studies with endothall-^{14}C in *Potamogeton nodosus* Poir. *Weed Res.*, vol. 8, p. 321-6.

Thompson, K. 1972. *Production studies on Cyperus papyrus in Lake George.* Roy. Soc. Symp. on Lake George, 4-8 September, London.

Thompson, K.; Gaudet, J. J. In press. A review of papyrus, and its role in tropical swamps.

Thomson, G. M. 1922. *The naturalisation of animals and plants in New Zealand.* Cambridge, Cambridge University Press. Cited by Chapman, 1970.

Thornton, I. 1957. Faunal succession in umbels of *Cyperus papyrus* L. on the Upper White Nile. *Proc. R. Ent. Soc. Lond.*, Ser A, vol. 32, p. 119-31.

Timmer, C. E.; Weldon, L. W. 1967. Evapotranspiration and pollution of water by water hyacinth. *Hyacinth Contr. J.*, vol. 6, p. 34-7.

Timmons, F. L. 1960. *Weed control in western irrigation and drainage systems.* Washington, D.C., Agric. Research Service, U.S. Dept. of Agric. and Bur. of Reclam., U.S. Dept. of the Interior, joint report. (ARS 34-14). Cited by Guscio *et al.* (1965).

Timmons, F. L.; Bruns, V. F.; Lee, W. O.; Yeo, R. R.; Hodgson, J. M.; Weldon, L. W.; Comes, R. D. 1963. *Studies on the control of common cattail in drainage canals and ditches.*

Washington, D.C., Agric. Research Service, U.S. Dept. of Agric. and Bur. of Reclam., U.S. Dept. of the Interior (Techn. Bull., no. 1286).

Timmons, F. L.; Frank, P. A.; Demint, R. J. 1969. Herbicide residues in agricultural water from control of aquatic and bank weeds. *Proc. Symp. Role of Agriculture in Clean Water.* Ames, Iowa, Iowa State University Press. (In press, est. October 1970).

Toth, S. J.; Riemer, D. N. 1968. Precise chemical control of algae in ponds. *J. Amer Water Works Ass.,* vol. 60, p. 367-71.

Tur, N. M. 1965. Un caso de epifitismo acuático. *Boln Soc. Argent. Bot.,* vol. 10, p. 323-7.

Tutin, T. 1941. The hydrosere and current concepts of the climax. *J. Ecol.,* vol. 29, p. 268-79.

United States Department of Agriculture. 1963. *Chemical control of submerged waterweeds in western irrigation and drainage canals.* 14 p. Joint Rep. with U.S. Dep. Interior, Bur. Reclam. (ARS 34-57).

van Donselaar, J. 1968. Water and marsh plants in the artificial Brokopondo Lake (Surinam, S. America) during the first three years of its existence. *Acta bot. neerl.,* vol. 17, p. 183-96.

Van Valin, C.C. 1966. Persistence of 2,6-dichlorobenzonitrile in aquatic environments. *Adv. in Chem.,* no. 60, p. 271-9. (Amer. Chem. Soc.).

Vogel, E.; Oliver, A. D. 1969. Evaluation of *Arzama densa* as an aid in the control of water hyacinth in Louisiana. *J. econ. Ent.,* vol. 62, p. 142-5.

Vollenweider, R. A. 1969. *A manual on methods for measuring primary production in aquatic environments.* Oxford, Blackwell, (IBP handbook, no. 12).

Wahlquist, H. 1972. Production of water hyacinths and resulting water quality in earthen ponds. *Hyacinth Contr. J.,* vol. 10, p. 9-11.

Walker, B. H. 1970. An evaluation of eight methods of botanical analysis on grasslands in Rhodesia. *J. appl. Ecol.,* vol. 7, p. 403-16.

Walker, C. R. 1963. Endothall derivatives as aquatic herbicides in fishery habitats. *Weeds,* vol. 11, p. 226-32.

— . 1964a. Simazine and other s-triazine compounds as aquatic herbicides in fish habitats. *Weeds,* vol. 12, p. 134-9.

— . 1964b. Dichlobenil (2,6-dichlorobenzonitrile) as a herbicide in fishery habitats. *Weeds,* vol. 12, p. 267-9.

— . 1965. Diuron, fenuron, monuron, neburon, and TCA mixtures as aquatic herbicides in fish habitats. *Weeds,* vol. 13, p. 296-301.

Ware, F. J. 1966. The use of copper sulfate as a method of partial control of elodea *(Elodea densa)* in Lake Thonotosassa, Florida. *Proc. So. Weed Conf.,* vol. 19, p. 491-4.

Watson, E. F. 1947. The utilisation of water hyacinth. *Handbook of utilization of aquatic plants,* p. 11-12. Edited by E. C. S. Little. Rome, Food and Agriculture Organization of the United Nations.

Watson, D. J. 1952. The physiological basis of variation in yield. *Adv. Agron.,* vol. 4, p. 101-45.

Watson, R.; Parker, I. 1970. The ecology of Lake Naivasha: the identification and description of some important components for a model. *Afr. Sci.,* vol. 2.

Watson, R.; Singh, T.; Parker, I. 1970. The diet of ducks and coot on Lake Naivasha. *E. Afr. Wildl. J.,* vol. 8, p. 131-44.

Way, J. M.; Newman, J. F.; Moore, N. W.; Knaggs, F. W. 1971. Some ecological effects of the use of paraquat for the control of weeds in small lakes. *J. appl. Ecol.,* vol. 8, p. 509-32.

Welch, P. S. 1948. *Limnological methods.* New York, McGraw-Hill.

— . 1952. *Limnology.* 2nd ed. New York, McGraw-Hill.

Weldon, L. W.; Blackburn, R. D. 1967. The control of floating aquatic weeds with ametryne. *Proc. So. Weed Conf.,* vol. 20, p. 312-18.

— . 1969. Herbicidal treatment effect on carbohydrate levels of alligatorweed. *Weed Sci.,* vol. 17, p. 66-9.

Weldon, L. W.; Blackburn, R. D.; Harrison, D. S. 1969. *Common aquatic weeds.* Washington, D.C., U.S. Govt. Printer, (Agric. Res. Service, U.S. Dept. Agric., Handbook, no. 352).

Westlake, D. F. 1959. The effects of biological communities on conditions in polluted streams. *The effects of pollution on living material,* p. 25-31. Edited by W. B. Yapp. London, Institute of Biology.

— . 1963. Comparisons of plant productivity. *Biol. Rev.,* vol. 38, p. 385-425.

— . 1965. Some basic data for investigations of the productivity of aquatic macrophytes. *Primary productivity in aquatic environments,* p. 231-48. Edited by C. Goldman. Berkeley, University of California Press, (Mem. 1st. Ital. Idrobiol., 18 (suppl.)).

— . 1968. The weight of water-weed in the River Frome. *Yb. Ass. River Auth,, 1968,* p. 3-12.

— . 1969. Primary production rates from changes in biomass-macrophytes. *A manual on methods for measuring primary production in aquatic environments,* p. 103-7. Edited by R. A. Vollenweider. Oxford, Blackwell. (IBP Handbook, no. 12).

Wetzel, R. 1960. Marl encrustation on hydrophytes in several Michigan lakes. *Oikos,* vol. 11, p. 223-8.

— . 1964. A comparative study of the primary productivity of higher aquatic plants, periphyton, and phytoplankton in a large, shallow lake. *Int. Revue ges. Hydrobiol. Hydrogr.,* vol. 49, p. 1-61.

— . 1969. Excretion of dissolved organic compounds by aquatic macrophytes. *Bioscience,* vol. 19, p. 539-40.

Wetzel, R.; Manny, B. 1971. Excretion of organic carbon and nitrogen. 18th Int. Limnol. Congress, Leningrad.

White, A. C. 1962. Diquat-prospective role in aquatic weed control. *Hyacinth Contr. J.,* vol. 1, p. 4.

— . 1965. Status report on diquat and paraquat as aquatic herbicides. *Hyacinth Contr. J.,* vol. 4, p. 18-19.

White, G. F. 1969. *Strategies of American water management.* Ann Arbor, University of Michigan Press.

Wild, H. 1961. Harmful aquatic plants in Africa and Madagascar. *Kirkia,* vol. 2, p. 1-66.

Wild, H.; Mitchell, D. S. 1970. The effect of Bayluscide on the water fern *Salvinia auriculata* and other aquatic plants. *Höfchenbr. Bayer PflSchutz-Nachr.,* vol. 23, p. 105-10.

Williams, R. F. 1946. The physiology of plant growth with special reference to the concept of net assimilation rate. *Ann. Bot.,* vol. 10, p. 41-72.

Williams, R. H. 1956. *Salvinia auriculata* Aublet: the chemical eradication of a serious aquatic weed in Ceylon. *Trop. Agric., Trin.,* vol. 33, p. 145-57.

Williams, W. D. 1969. Eutrophication of lakes. Symposium: the aquatic environment and man. *Proc. R. Soc. Vict.,* vol. 83, p. 17-26.

Wilson, C. L. 1969. Use of pathogens in weed control. *A. Rev. Phytopath.,* vol. 7, p. 411-34.

Wilson, Dennis C.; Bond, C. E. 1969. The effects of the herbicide diquat and dichlobenil on pond invertebrates. *Trans. Amer. Fish. Soc.,* vol. 98, p. 438-43.

Yeo, R. R. 1964. Life history of common cattail. *Weeds,* vol. 12, p. 284-8.

— . 1967. Silver dollar fish for biological control of submersed aquatic weeds. *Weeds,* vol. 15, p. 27-31.

— . 1967. Dissipation of diquat and paraquat and effects on aquatic weeds and fish. *Weeds,* vol. 15, p. 42-6.

Yeo, R. R.; Fisher, T. W. 1970. *Progress and potential for biological weed control with fish, pathogens, competitive plants, and snails.* Rome, (Italy) FAO Int. Conf. Weed Control.

Younger, R. 1958. Preliminary studies using kuron as an aquatic herbicide. *Proc. No. East. Weed Contr. Conf.,* vol. 12, p. 332-7.

Yount, J. L.; Crossman, R. A. 1970. Eutrophication control by plant harvesting. *J. Wat. Pollut. Control Fed.,* vol. 42, p. 173-83.

Zettler, F. W.; Freeman, T. E.; Rentz, R. E.; Hill, H. R. 1971. Plant pathogens with potential for biological control of water hyacinth and alligator weed. Paper presented at the 11th Annual Meeting Hyacinth Control Society, Tampa, Fla., July 1971.

Zwölfer, H..; Harris, P. 1971. Host specificity determination of insects for biological control of weeds. *A. Rev. Ent.,* vol. 16, p. 159-78.

Index of organisms

Index of herbicides

IMPRIMERIE LOUIS-JEAN
Publications scientifiques et littéraires
TYPO - OFFSET

05002 GAP - Téléphone 51-35-23 +

Dépôt légal 51 - 1974